Hindsight is 2020.
Two years that prove truth can be stranger than fiction.

    This story was written in hopes of helping us put our differences aside as a species and shedding light on the years that shook up our existence.

    There is something here that can keep us connected, keep us humble.

    To my family and my friends who I will always hold dear,

    To you… as my reader,

You are important, you are enough, and you are part of this.

    To all of those who have helped shape this story, to those who have been impacted…

    Thank you for your journey.

Enjoy the book!
Love you so much...
Always,
Jill (and Nikki)

~*~ Prologue ~*~

This story and how it came to be is one of a kind. Fictional stories are entertaining, mind bending, educational and can be somewhat realistic... this story you hold in your hands is all of those things...but different - because it's true.

Non-fiction that is most definitely stranger than fiction. It stems from me, branches across the world, and reaches you. We are all connected.

~*~The Awakening~*~

As I groaned in pain, I mentioned, "my phone always rings off the hook while I'm in a massage, I will never understand that phenomena." Sam, my therapist, giggled. Was that laugh because of my phone blowing up in my purse? Or because of her insanely deep tissue massage that had me writhing in pain? It hurt like a bitch every time, but I needed it badly, so I would push through the 120 minutes every month or so.

I came into the lobby more relaxed than I was expecting to be, after a deep tissue beatdown. . .

You would be surprised at how quickly moods can change.

I should mention this was my place of work as the general manager.

As I handed Mel, the receptionist, my debit card, I simultaneously looked at my phone.
"Where are you?
The apartment is flooding…..
BRING PAPER TOWELS, BABE!
Help!!!
Where are you?!!!"

My screen was filled with single messages, seconds apart, 9 missed calls and a couple of miscellaneous emails. All made themselves known as I scrolled my screen.

"I am so sorry, I have to go, I left my tip with Sam. Am I all settled, did you give me my card back?" She nodded, eyes wide at my frantic manor.

Once I hit the pavement, I called my man.

"Babe, what the hell is happening?!" He followed with a jumble of words that are not worth writing out, but if it helps, my response was... "Babe, if I stop for paper towels, I won't be home for at least a half an hour! Why don't you dump out the pots and reuse them?! Ring the towels out!" He paused in disbelief that he had not thought of that.

Pulling up to my building, there were restoration trucks taking up the whole street. As I squeezed through and pulled into the garage, I could see a pathway of wet concrete from the stairwell to the drains. I noticed a towel in my car so I wrapped it around my neck and headed up the stairs that had water streaming down them from above.

We lived on the 2nd floor and the stairs got more and more wet as I ascended. When I opened the door to my hallway and stepped on the carpet, it was like that gross, squishy fake grass they have at water parks. The restoration company had its minions scrambling the hallways, men in pink shirts, I might add. I opened my apartment door to find Carter, my man, sitting on the couch. It looked like it was the first time he had been able to sit for hours, his eyes widened and he jumped up the second I entered.

Towels were blanketed on the ground and every pot and bowl-like object in the house was on the floor catching water.

One single, skinny stream was what caught my attention first. It was dropping from the breakfast bar light fixture. The other light had a steady drip too!

Then, as I looked around, I noticed there were pots sitting under the other lights in the kitchen, the smoke detector and underneath the fire sprinkler system!

"What the hell happened?!!!" I shrieked, lifting and dumping a full pot in the sink and immediately replacing it under the dripping fixture.

The couch was surprisingly dry, so we sat for a moment. Carter took a deep breath before diving into the afternoon's shenanigans!

"Well, I was just chilling when the fire alarm started going off. As usual, I put my headphones on and covered Mia's ears."

"Good thing I got you those noise canceling headphones last Christmas, huh? What about Kalypso?! He is probably deaf now!" I joked. I will quickly introduce our kitties, Kalypso and Mia. Kalpyso is a fluffy, white, spunky Siberian and Mia is a talkative, blind, independent Calico.

"So I was sitting there with the fire alarm going off for... like forever. When it finally stopped, I took the headphones off and that's when... I heard the dripping."

His eyes expanded. He stood up in dramatic fashion and went on, "It started over here." He stood at the kitchen island.

"Then I saw that it was coming out of all the holes in the ceiling! Then I noticed the floor, water was slowly headed for the carpet in the room... like the blob or something! I grabbed towels and started setting them out... then put the pots down. Babe, this is crazy! They're going to have to do some serious work on the building now. Look at the bubbles in the ceiling..." He pointed up. Sure enough, there were two... and they were growing. We looked at each other, and a touch of dread set in.

"I can't believe you were supposed to work today and gave the hours away. Imagine if neither of us were home! That was really lucky, divine intervention!" I looked at him, shaking my head. We both knew how much worse it would have been, and tried not to let our imaginations go there.

It took part of this whole story to realize, but there was a lot of divine intervention working here. This was all just beginning to unfold, if we only knew to what extent. Buckle up, readers!

Right then, someone knocked.

Together, we went and opened the door. The property managers stood there, dumbfounded. I looked at them, my eyes questioning what the hell was going on. They explained that someone stole a piece of the water suppression system in the stairwell on the 3rd floor. I felt my left eyebrow rise, then the right one followed as I registered what they had just said. That's all they could tell us.

They asked us if we were ok to stay in our apartment overnight, to which we agreed. They then left us only wanting to know more about the situation.

The next morning while I was at work, Carter made himself an omelet. He was on a serious kick at the time, but he was interrupted by the pink-shirted minions right as he was ready to eat.

After a quick explanation of needing to dehumidify the walls and ceiling, they began rolling in big pieces of junky-looking equipment.

It all happened so fast, like a flash. Fans were placed, cords ran, taped down, plugged in and turned on.

Dust bunnies came out of their long-time hiding places and went straight for Carter's breakfast. *Savages.*

"Woah, woah, WOAH!!" Carter threw his omelet in the microwave to protect it, "Bro! Turn those off."

"Hey man, I know this is a lot to take in," Pink started to say, "but we have to put these fans down to

dehumidify the building. They need to be running for at least the next 24-48. Sorry bro."
He wasn't sorry.

Carter looked at him, "Obviously I understand what's happening here… but I was literally just about to sit down for breakfast. I am keeping them off while I do that. I get they need to be on. Do you guys have any info about what kind of work needs to be done here? How long is all of that going to take?"
They all looked both ways at each other, figuring out who should speak.

"We don't really have any of that info yet, but we will definitely let you know when we know more. We gotta let the building dry out before we can look."

Without any other conversation, the guys went silent and awkwardly walked out. Carter paused for a second, looking at the fans and dehumidifiers taking over the kitchen and living room. I would be willing to bet there was a rub of his temples, a forceful sigh and a hand through his hair before he took another step.

~*~

Over the next couple of days, the pink shirts came in and out, with various people explaining the same things. We questioned if there were 2 different companies with pink shirted workers… or absolutely no communication between higher ups. After each visit, we would just shake our heads at each other in disbelief of what was happening and how it seemed like nothing was going to get done.

We realized we might need to start thinking about moving… It was daunting.
Early in the morning, after we initially thought about a move, we were informed that they were probably going to need to take the ceiling down in the apartment. I got on the "interwebs" right away and researched what was out there for possible immediate move-in.
If you have never had to move in quick fashion, consider yourself lucky.

After a couple days of calling, visiting and applying, we were all set to move into a nice little apartment with 2 rooms and 2 balconies. We were just waiting for the go-ahead from the leasing office on background checks.
Carter worked in the music industry, packing the artists' trucks and setting up their staging. He loves it!

Lucky for us, he was able to make his own schedule to be able to be home for all of the dudes coming in and out.

He and all of his coworkers were also basically glorified movers, so he had some of his work crew come over to help us move. They brought dollies and a pimped-out, circus short-bus! We loaded the bus up in no time, and waited for the leasing office's call that we were good to start moving in.

Waiting turned into dinner time, which came with a main course of frustration. *Was there something wrong with one of our background checks? Were we not going to get the apartment? We just did all this packing, do we have to unpack it now?*

We ended up not hearing anything from them that evening. Thankfully, the guys and their bus lived in a safe place, so we sent them home with most of our stuff packed up in the bus. We were hoping to hear from the leasing office in the morning and we would hit them up at that point.

They didn't call us. For the whole day…

At this point, the circus bus crew needed their vehicle and had to bring our stuff back into our apartment. *What a bust!*

Carter and I ended up visiting another apartment complex the next morning. They welcomed us in, gave us hot cappuccino and a tour of the very beautiful, brand-new, and totally empty building. It was like a 5-star country club! Equipped with a pool and hot tub, gym, game and poker room, business center, coffee bar, and sky decks with top-chef quality grills...we were sold.

You know how that goes though... a new building equals higher rent. Once we saw the apartment we were going to be in, we knew that we wanted to live there. Even if it would make us go broke, we both had good jobs... and needed to move quickly so our ceiling didn't cave in on us. *Did we really have a choice?*

The layout was almost exactly the same as our old place, but everything was shiny and new. The lighting was exceptional, and the kitchen was exactly what we needed. We were about to level up our cooking game, no doubt. Everything was perfect, so we started the application process and began the waiting game for the background checks...again. We went home with bated breath.

We sat in our living room, surrounded by a city of leaning box towers and bags of various items. All of our life was sitting stacked up around us, out of the way of the now dripping ceiling. The bubbles continued to slowly grow, and as the fans whirled, the dust bunnies danced in celebration of their freedom. *We gotta get outta here!*

I got an email from the apartment complex. We were good to start moving in the next day, after the lease signing. I set an appointment to do it first thing in the morning.

The next day, one of Carter's stage hands, Sean, had agreed to help us move with his box truck. We sprung out of bed and got the lease signing done. Easy-peasy! Sean met us outside our apartment, dollies in hand. These guys move shit for a living, so they don't mess around! We took the first load out to the truck, methodically. I let Carter take the lead on this process, knowing he would bust it out like a show day truck loading.

When I say that these guys were glorified movers, I had no idea what a skill it was until this move. Carter and the guys unload and then re-pack semi's for bands like Dead & Company, Slayer, Bob Dylan and many more greats, really any band that came through Denver... They were the guys. They have this whole truck packing thing down to an art. Carter had our stuff lined up in our apartment. First stuff into the truck would come out last on wheels, and then packing the other stuff around it.

I had never thought of packing the bottom of tables, he TETRIS'd the bottom of the coffee table like a pro-gamer. That came out of the truck all in one unit and straight onto the dolly. Up the ramp, through the hall and into the apartment, repeat. I was loving this. Game changing!

***Disclaimer:** keep up with my tangents throughout this story, wild memories come up day after day about the year.

Mid-load, the phone rang. Carter grabbed it, "Whassup Willie?!" He turned and spoke with him, pacing on the sidewalk by the truck. After the call he walked back up to us with a blank face.

"So, the show at The Mission (a venue in Denver) just got canceled 'cuz of the virus." All of us paused for a second, frozen.

Let me rewind… Tangent, commence.

~*~

This story begins in March of 2020. If you're still not recalling what happened in 2020 because you either blacked it out of your memory or you're so enthralled with this unraveling story... 2020 was a straight dumpster fire. This is just my own true account of the year. One that was, quite frankly, stranger than a fictional story.

On January 2nd, 2020, news broke that there were horrible bushfires in Australia. Over 400 separate fires burning, pushing animals and people out of homes and off land. These fires devoured over 46 million acres of land across Australia, destroying thousands of buildings and taking the lives of many from both direct impact, and afterwards due to smoke inhalation.

There were apocalyptic photos, with people and native wildlife huddling together on beaches, as flames engulfed everything around them. There was tragedy captured in other images. We won't go into it... but being an animal lover, I was devastated.

Ok, so fires in Australia to ring in the new year. Less than a week later, news stories started reporting about a "mysterious pneumonia" outbreak that was happening in China. Novel Coronavirus, or COVID-19 was born. Airborne.

It was apparently spread by intercepting a cough or sneeze of an infected person, or by touching them or surfaces they've touched! Before you could even say "coronavirus, what?"... BOOM...It was in almost every country! Social media spewed misinformation. Conspiracies started to get loose, running wildly like prison escapees through communities... just like the virus.

Oh, if we only knew. More on COVID to come, hang in there with me...

To polish off only the first month of this hellish year, legendary basketball star Kobe Bryant died with his daughter in a suspicious helicopter crash! Kobe and his daughter Gianna, along with 7 others were killed. People didn't believe that it happened, thinking that the story was fraudulent, staged or planned out to kill the Bryant name. It was pretty devastating. The questions surrounding the crash almost muted the sad words of Kobe's widow as she gave her speech at the memorial, which had me crying.

I remember so clearly in high school playing Beer Pong and anytime someone would do the layup throw, everyone would yell "Kobe!" *Salute, rest in peace. May the court be your sanctuary, the ball be your wings.*

I promise this story has some good in it, but like the writings of Lemony Snicket, the author of The Series of Unfortunate Events, you must know that this story is not sunshine and rainbows. There is darkness and sadness in this endeavor you've started here, but it's a good mind blow to the shit-show that was 2020. All true.

In February, there was an impeachment trial against our orange government tyrant. Donald Trump had been wreaking havoc for years, even before he was elected president... and 2020 just had to fall on an election year. It seemed like the impeachment news came and went... nothing ever happened... The dude was still in office, still president. I was starting to question my knowledge of the definition of the word "impeach".

Hmmm, nope. Straight from Merriam-Webster Dictionary:

<u>*Impeach: [verb]*</u> *to bring an accusation against, to remove from office especially for misconduct.*

So... why was he still in office?

I am not one for politics, in fact, when it comes up in conversations, I either mentally block what's being said, or move to another room. However, throughout this story you will read of my thoughts and encounters on things that happened that just make this story that much crazier.

Again, the truth can be stranger than fiction... and this story's goal is to prove that to you. Everything in this book is 100% true life shit.

Now, let's continue.

As a short recap of the first 8 weeks of the year, we have one of the largest bushfires in history happening in Australia, this weird ass virus starting to make itself known, death of a sports legend, and an unsuccessful impeachment of the U.S. president.

That brings us back to March… The news was starting to turn back to Covid-19 and its severity, but meanwhile, my apartment is flooding. That happened on only the 4th day in March.

~*~

We reconvened at the truck, where we had just learned that the first, of many, concerts had been canceled. On the bright side, Willie and the guys were on their way over with more hands and wheels to help us move!

They come barreling into the building, 12 pack of Corona Extra in hand. Willie joked that he was "feeling like getting Corona". A joke that shouldn't have been funny, but was.

Corona beer would end up taking a pretty negative hit for the next few months as Coronavirus dominated the world and the news. Not a financial hit, as many were thinking just like Willie, but a big public relations hit just because of the "similarity in name". *People are so ridiculous.*

Our entire apartment, with 2.5 years of memories... and that much shit, went into the truck and out, 3 times over and we were done. Our last load was our cars full of art and our 2 kitties, Kalypso and Mia. We unloaded our cars onto the dollies, stacked the fur babies, and wheeled in the last of our treasures.

We...crushed...it!

We all loaded up and headed to the closest burger joint, starving. Carter ordered a nacho appetizer and it came like a tortilla, nacho, torta stack. A nacho skyscraper really!

Each of us ordered a different burger, I couldn't even tell you what they all were, but I will never forget mine. Veggie and black bean burger with green chilies and pepper jack on a warm Brioche bun with sweet potato tots. *Are you drooling yet?*

We talked about the last shows they all had worked at, and I just sat there listening to the industry jargon thinking about **what** my next show would be, or **when** it would be...

Literally, as I was thinking that, I was pulled out of thought by the word "postponed". The guys already knew, they were being informed about gigs that had already been pushed back because of the virus. Of course you can't have thousands of people crammed into a concert venue, shoulder to shoulder... someone is bound to have been exposed before they attended the show. That's how rampant this thing was. Exposures became the worst news you could ever get, of course besides actually testing positive yourself.

It's really hard to explain in words, but I truly think that the entire world did not even know what was happening. We definitely were not expecting, or prepared for, what was about to happen. No one knew the severity of coronavirus yet, but it was soon to come sweeping the world by storm.

I started writing this for you in 2021 and for this entire year, I have truly tried to wrap my head around how much happened. An image came to mind.
The image of an evil four year old with a magnifying glass between the sun and the earth trying to eradicate humanity! A grim thought, at that!

By the time we got home from dinner, not even 2 hours later, we had already learned about yet another concert that was being canceled… the one I realized I was supposed to go to next. *Of course.*
I could see the anxiety in Carter's eyes about the shows being canceled. That was his livelihood, his passion, his career!
"I hope this thing comes and goes quickly," Carter said.

There was another task that needed to be done this evening before we could really rest. Cleaning supplies and a few other things needed to come from the old apartment. We drove over there and took the front stairs because the elevator was taking forever.

There wasn't much to grab, but it was still a couple loads. I gathered up as much as I could carry and held the door for Carter, who carried a big box of glasses. We were lucky enough to have a stairwell right next to our apartment, but it was the one that flooded, so it now sat gutted, waiting to be redone after the water damage. The light was apparently broken in the stairwell... and it was pitch black. I lit up my phone and walked Carter down the stairs first, empty handed. Turning the corner something knocked me on the head. I looked with the light to see a hanging light fixture, wired to the ceiling with a **broken** lightbulb inside.

"Dude what the f**k?! This could seriously hurt someone, falling down the stairs from the darkness or getting their face slit open by broken glass! They're asking for a lawsuit here!"

Carter made it to the bottom, moving like a sloth around the destruction. While we ran another sketchy load, I was continuously stunned at how dangerous it was for people to be having to move like this. The stairs were pitch black, the hanging lightbulb, building supplies, itchy insulation and drywall created an obstacle course that I was running blind, whilst carrying breakable stuff. I should level up in my game of life for making it out of there unscathed.

All we had to do was take out the trash and turn in the keys in the morning and we could walk away from this craziness. Our complex was in for a long recovery.

When we walked into our new apartment, I was pleasantly surprised and grateful that our bed was already set up. *Smart move, boys...smart move.*

Thankfully, with our efficient moving methods, I knew right where the clothes were. More specifically the PJ's. In no time, I was out like the broken light in the stairwell we left behind.

My shift didn't start until 2:30 the next day so we got up early and went to the old apartment. We had just left the trash, some towels and a box of pens that probably only 50% contained ink.

When we walked in, the hallway was torn up from top to bottom, puking pink insulation from every orifice. Our apartment door was open, plastic hung like curtains. I opened one slowly to see guys in white hazmat suits tearing open the entire ceiling from the door to the far window. There was dust, insulation and drywall covering every inch of the place. They pointed to our stuff in the 2nd room. We covered our faces with our shirts and trudged through the grime. I left the trash bag, just swiped the towels and pens... and said a small, silent goodbye to the place we had enjoyed for a chapter.

Walking up to the elevator, 2 guys were waiting with a huge TV box on a skateboard. Their amateur dollie made me feel good about the efficiency of our move. In front of them was a couple arguing about carrying a dresser down the stairs because the elevator wasn't working. The next closest stairwell was across the building... and they didn't have any wheels.

We looked at each other, knowing the state of the deadly stairwell, thankful that we weren't in the same position as these guys. When we got down the stairs with our stuff, we took a moment of gratitude for the fact that we had acted quickly about moving and made it happen. This is one of those divine intervention moments I mentioned earlier... We were just hours ahead of the game.

People were now on top of each other trying to quickly uproot their lives and move all their shit out around drywall and insulation, uprooted carpet, cords and machinery. Not to mention the work crews and, oh yea... a broken elevator, forcing them to possibly use a stairwell that could potentially kill them... or lugging belongings across the entire complex!

Turning in our keys felt so good, the only worry left was getting our deposits back. It was a worry at first, but it came in time. We were 4 days into the month of March when the flood happened so we fought for our full month of rent back, plus the security and pet deposits!

At the spa the next morning, the energy was hectic. News was coming in that the 2020 Olympics was officially postponed because of COVID-19. And... that the World Health Organization had declared the Coronavirus a **global** pandemic. They were saying that potentially **70%** of the world's population could be infected by this deadly virus. We were being inundated by statistics, symptoms, outbreaks and more. This was just the start.

It figures that this would be an Olympics and Election year! A one in four chance.

~*~

I received a call from Carter's brother, who works in Washington D.C. ...*doing what? I am not allowed to know, fascinating!* Anyway, he said that things were going to be shut down nationwide. We needed to spread the word to loved ones and within our workplaces. I ended up informing my own boss it was coming, which she was later grateful for... but did not take it seriously at the moment.

We were going to have to close down the spa for a while, that was just the reality of the situation. I saw a newsreel about grocery stores running out of essential items and telling everyone to stock up on food and supplies for a 2 week lockdown.

I made sure I had energy to go to the store that night, but we needed more than 2 weeks, having just moved. There wasn't a single solid item of food in our fridge, just the condiments we saved from the flood zone.

In the grocery, rows and rows of shelves were completely empty. Toilet paper was an out-of-stock item **nationwide**, along with Clorox wipes and hand sanitizer. Canned foods were running low, ramen and pasta were hot items, too. Toilet paper though?!! As far as we knew, Covid-19 didn't cause insane amounts of explosive poops. Why did people need a car full? It was only a matter of time before a notice was sent out that you could not return those purchased items and that only **one pack** per household ws allowed. It felt like a solid dose of karma to those who bought $1000 worth of hand sanitizer, then stuck with it. *Suckers.*

    Making the best of the situation, anything on the shelves was going in the cart. Gratitude filled me that my mom made me eat fruits and veggies growing up, so I was not a picky eater. The American diet proved itself that night, as the produce section remained plenished and frozen dinners and boxed mac-n-cheese were nowhere to be found. *Any food in my belly and I'm happy.* The lady at the check-out looked at us like we were "doomsdayers", people who are always preparing for the apocalypse, even when it wasn't happening. Our cart held well over 2 weeks of food, so it made sense that she looked at us like we were crazies. I felt the need to mention that we had just moved a couple days before… she gave the *"yeah...right"* look.

    On the following day, we were told that bars and restaurants were closing, along with personal services, which meant the spas, tattoo parlors, hair and nail joints. Basically, anything and everything you could do in Denver was now closed. This city is known for its music scene, bars and food joints… and tattoos of course. Coloradans LOVE our tats.

    There was an official "Stay-At-Home" order in place. This was really to keep the hospitals from getting overcrowded and healthcare workers being so stretched thin that no one would get care! You were only allowed to leave for essentials, and only "essential businesses" were allowed to remain open.

We were officially on lockdown.

Something I think would be worth mentioning is the whole "essential business" thing. When the order came out to shut businesses down, people were lining the streets to stock up on booze and weed. The state government then changed course and came out with a notice that liquor stores and weed dispensaries were now deemed "essential businesses".

A day to celebrate as the war on drugs rages on, Colorado holding it down for the potheads and drinkers. I thought it was ironic that buying weed, which was once illegal to even have on you, was now an essential business for survival in a global pandemic. But then again, *good luck making people stay in their homes and taking away their beer and pot!*

~*~

On my final day of work at the spa, there was a lot to do. We had no clue how long we would be closed. There were roughly 250 appointments that needed to be canceled, so I stuck Kaitlyn and Mel on it. We needed to make sure all the laundry was done, and bags of sheets were by the back door for pick up. Holly got that job because she got to listen to music. Cynthia got the job of cleaning out the fountain and I went to help her vacuum the water out. The shop vac switch label was rubbed off so when I stuck the end in the fountain and turned it on, it blew out stagnant water all over me. After successfully extracting the water out, we got a giggle out of it, but I definitely stunk for the rest of the afternoon.

One thing you should know about me is that I am not, by any means, a girly girl. If that water had gotten on any other employee, it wouldn't have been a giggle fest. Everything happens for a reason, I guess.

The owner worked on getting me set up to work from home, to care for our 1,200 members who would **definitely** be calling with questions. I set a new voicemail for clients and tested out the call forwarding. I got log-in info for remote point-of-sale and closed out and emptied the register drawers.

While the girls were finishing up the list of tasks, I double checked that nothing could catch fire and burn the entire strip mall down. I locked the safe, turned off all the lights, locked the door and left the spa for the next 2 months. Though, in that moment, I didn't know when I would set foot in the spa again.

My house flooded on March 4th, our first night in our new apartment was on the 16th, and the spa and city closed down on the 19th. This year was starting to seem like a weird plot to a movie, or book, or maybe both!

Working from home was great. I still had to get up earlier than I would like, but you would be surprised how easy it is to roll out of bed, log in to work… and then wake up, start coffee and begin the day. I am a hardcore introvert and homebody by nature, this was going to ruin me. *It did.*

Kalypso would come and brush his tail against me and lay on the bed I made him next to the desk. He would lay there all day, enjoying the spa vibe I had brought home with me. Tranquil music kept the chill-vibe strong, though I was able to listen to the artists that I actually like in that genre. I got some aromatherapy going, opened up the windows, and got in the zone every day. Would you believe I even had a mug warmer for my tea, a foot massager, and a boyfriend who had nothing better to do than cook me breakfast-at-desk?!!

Every so often Kalypso would wake up from a nap and sleepwalk onto the desk, step onto my chest and lie down, shoving his perfect head into my neck and stretching down my whole upper half. Fifteen pounds of pure joy. How was I supposed to get anything done, let alone...ever leave my house to work again. *I was ruined.*

As the weeks went by, I kept my employees engaged as much as I could, ensuring they were still on the payroll and would have a job when we reopened. The questions were frequent, both from employees and paying members. My phone rang off the hook as they wondered if they would be charged, how to stop their recurring payment, when we would reopen, what services we would offer, and a variety of other things that had no definitive answer. Thankfully, I had been with the spa long enough to learn how to maneuver around the system and help them remain confident that we had their best interests in mind.

These were uncharted waters for everyone. I had to remind myself, and them, of that often. Upon reopening, the members came to refer to me as the queen of customer service. I took it, proud that I could help them out in this time of uncertainty.

~*~

    My aunt called one day in early April, informing our family of an incident that happened within her company, in which crazy shit happens all the time! So, when she called, I didn't know what to expect.
    Quick tangent: My aunt took over my uncle's tugboat company in south Florida after he passed away. It was something she never, in a million years, thought she would be doing. My uncle was known as the "King of the Miami River", his tugboat company known well throughout the southern East Coast states. When he passed away, my aunt decided she needed to keep his legacy going, especially since the company and earnings were supposed to go to my cousins.
    With her bright and sharp-witted mind, she has since been crushing the Tugboat game, which is a completely male dominated industry! There have been more than a few articles and Q&A's done with her now… being the (quoting Game of Thrones here) "Queen-mother of the Miami River". She took over the throne, in other words.

    Anyway, she explained that on one of the trips from Haiti to Miami, stow-aways had hidden in the tires! If you've never seen a tugboat, these tires are tractor size, and act as fenders on the sides of the boat…lining the entire hull... which could crush a human with "trash-compactor" like force as they hit the docks. These dudes got lucky that the captain approached the dock slowly, how it should be... and they jumped out and made a quick getaway onto the streets of Miami. This story happens all too often on boats coming and going from the islands, but this was the first my aunt had experienced it. She was a bit shaken, but the spirit of my uncle was at her back, and still is... among all the crazy situations that still continue to arise.

    Throughout Covid, she had to navigate through the ever changing crew. They live on the boats in really close quarters. Exposures were running high and she would need to act quickly if someone had exposure or even simply wasn't feeling well. Stress levels run high in that industry anyway, Covid didn't help anything... not that it helped any industry.

~*~

My best friend, Becca, called me one night and told me that she was putting together an Easter egg scavenger hunt for her boyfriend, and at the end of it she was going to propose to him! She had spent the last couple weeks carving 2 rings and a box out of Aspen Tree wood. When she sent me the picture, I squealed. She had burned a heart and "Love Always" into the lid of the box. I helped her put clues together for the scavenger hunt and she read me what she had written for the proposal. I cried like a baby. Thankfully, he said YES!

This girl is everything to me, and now we would be planning her wedding! She had been through her fair share of shitty boyfriends, and this guy was *the one*. He was nothing like the guys she had dated in the past, and both of us knew this was the guy for her for the long haul.

I hated the way that her past relationships always ended. There was one that we literally had to shove him out packing, back to his home state. One jumped off of our 3rd floor balcony as the cops barged in after him. Another struggled with addiction that spun out of control quickly. He, unfortunately, lost his battle. *Rest in Peace, Mikey.*

We're not going to go any further on that subject because they aren't part of our future story, but I was protective of her, to say the least. This current guy officially had my full stamp of approval. I would fight to help them protect their *happily-forever-after*.

After her successful proposal, she asked me to be her maid-of-honor. There was no question necessary, but I was ecstatic to accept the offer. We were going to make this the perfect day for her, she deserved it. Over the course of the year, we would spend hours talking about her wedding plan, in giddy fashion. I never realized how much work planning a wedding was, but being with my best friend, it remained fun.

~*~

The stay-at-home order continued through April, as COVID ravaged its way through the country...and the world. My work days were running together, but I was grateful to be safe in my fortress with my little family.

It was actually kind of comical that all the Colorado stoners were so excited for April of this year! Denver usually has a whole weekend of 4/20 festivities and concerts... *"a whole month of 4/20 bro, 4/20/2020!"* and we were all quarantined during it. That's some bad stoner karma, if you ask me! However, good thing Pot Shops were still open and *essential* to *survival*!

Later in April, the White House and presidential figures revealed that UFO's and other life-forces were REAL. They revealed that there was a whole archive of evidence of extraterrestrial life. *Hallelujah!* I had always believed that we couldn't be the only life force in the galaxy... but now we would be able to believe freely. That was huge!

Although we were stoked about this news being released, we realized that it could have been a ploy to turn the news to another side of the government... *Were our "leaders" releasing this news to turn our heads away from how badly they had reacted to the pandemic? Was this development made public right now for a reason that wasn't fully being disclosed? Why NOW?*

Either way, we knew now, that we wouldn't be thought of as crazy for believing in aliens. That was something to celebrate! More information would develop as time went on and more evidence was released by both the public and government.

~*~

Moving forward with the craziness that is 2020...

    May 1st was a calm and warm spring night. Carter and I were watching a movie called Extraction. I only feel the need to say the name, because if you've seen it, you know it's got a LOT of gunfire and is a pretty loud movie in general. If you haven't seen it, be prepared to be turning the volume up and down throughout the whole thing... as the voices and gunfire volume do not flow whatsoever.
    Anyway, there was a moment that we had to pause for a call I had to take for work. It was a quick call, but the second I hung up the phone our night went from calm to crazy faster than you can say "Extraction"!
    "Get on the ground!" Followed by 4 gunshots right outside our apartment.
    I looked out the window to see a police officer with his gun still raised. Looking just past him was a man on the ground, face down, not moving. The officer took a few steps forward and kicked a gun that was on the ground, as another officer ran over to the man who had been shot down.
    They flipped him over and began the first steps of CPR, but quickly stopped, then lifted him into an ambulance that arrived a few minutes later. It seemed to

me that they knew he was already gone, being that they did not continue the CPR.

Carter and I stood there in shock, peering out the window while trying not to stare. In the moments following, our whole block was flooded with police, fire trucks, multiple ambulances and crime scene investigation personnel. They taped off the area. Residents of our building, and the neighboring buildings, stood on their balconies watching the whole thing go down. I felt myself wondering if anyone had seen the piece we had just seen. The officer had just shot that man in the back 4 times! **In the back!** I thought to myself, *what the hell could that poor man have done to be shot down from behind?!*

The scene went on late into the night, with officers and CSI standing around looking at each other in the taped off area. I was having a hard time wrapping my mind around it.

I'm a small-town mountain girl. I had never seen anything like this. I guess I was in the big city now and not liking the feeling I had in my gut. Danger and the feeling of not being safe in my own home sent nightmarish thoughts through my head.

The following day, I was determined to find out about the man who had been shot down. Turns out, police had been trying to locate his car since early evening because of suspicious activity and driving at high speeds, possibly in a stolen car. They had finally located him and the vehicle. When he tried to run, he half turned and pointed a handgun towards the officer, the officer shot him.

The next morning, there was blood on the ground where he was shot, which solidified that what we had witnessed the night before had really happened and was not just a bad dream.

As I sat at my desk that afternoon, I saw a car pull up and park right in front of where he had fallen. They placed a bouquet of flowers and a balloon at the spot where he had been shot. A woman sat down, right in the middle of the road, and wept. I wished so badly I could go hug her. I could feel her despair, her heartbreak, from where I sat. *Was she his wife, sister or friend? I guess it didn't matter.*

I watched her for a while and sent a prayer her way that she would find peace. She left the balloon hovering as the sun went down. There was no wind. The red, heart-shaped balloon just hung there, with his spirit. I could feel him there. My eyes hung, too, watching the balloon slowly turn and swoop.

Shortly after, a car drove up. It stopped in front of the temporary headstone and I realized that the balloon had been placed in the middle of the street. The car paused and then slowly went around it, careful not to sway the balloon out of place. The woman came back the next morning and planted a flower garden on the corner near where he was killed. Those are still blooming today, letting

his spirit live on, letting him be seen and remembered by all of us who surround that corner.
Rest in Peace. Gone but not forgotten.

~*~

We now sit in the middle of May, and I know this story has been heavy and has been A LOT. There is still much to come, but picture this…

At this point in the pandemic, people were starting to crave their personal services, more specifically, nails and haircuts. The internet was flooding with people trying to do their own salon quality nails and even cut their own bangs! You can imagine how those came out…

Carter decided that he trusted me enough to cut his hair….and choose the style for his face! People's hairstyles were starting to go viral online and this one should have, but I was denied that permission.

I brushed Carter's hair out while it was wet from a shower, grabbed the scissors, and cut a straight line across his back. Easy. When he grabbed his shaver, I started buzzing down one side of his face. I had never tried to buzz a boyfriend's face before, so I was nervous. I did one line, freaked out and let him complete the task. When he came and found me, his entire face was shaved… except one small spot of hair on his jaw line. Not on both sides, just one.

The only comparison I can give you is, at first glance, it looked like a mole. He gave me one statuesque pose and I quickly snapped a picture... the one I was denied sharing with the world.

At least it could live in my own archives, to be enjoyed and laughed at forever more.

~*~

A few days later, on May 17th, I was lucky enough to celebrate 3 years sober from alcohol. At that moment I was supposed to be on a plane to Madrid to meet my mom.

When I was a sophomore in high school, we had a wonderful young woman stay with us as an exchange student, Carla. I had gone back to Spain with her years earlier, in 2007, and was so looking forward to seeing her again. My mom would be finishing up a bicycle trip through Belgium and Amsterdam. Unfortunately, that was one of many trips that Covid so rudely disrupted. I spent hours trying to persuade the airline for that money back, with success after some badass, executive-level debate.

I spent that day reminiscing about my 2-year sober celebration. The year before, my mom and I had traveled to Peru and spent a week doing Yoga and exploring the Sacred Valley. We hiked to Inca ruins, learned about their genius creations for growing food, and saw how the people have carried their ways into today, even with some still speaking only the native tongue of the Inca people, called "Quechua".

The most divine thing had happened. When you plan your trip, you have to register for the day you want to visit the world wonder, Machu Picchu. It just so happened that our fearless leader had registered us for May 17th, without even knowing the specialness of that date!

    I'd like to take a moment to tell you about that day. I could write a whole book on our trip to Peru. Maybe that will come later, but I want to tell you about the day at Machu Picchu before we continue.

    We woke up in our hotel at 4am to get on the bus to the world wonder. I have never in my life woken up that easily, that early in the morning. My eyes popped open to my mom piddling around the room, quiet as a mouse. The second she saw me awake, she sat on her bed and handed me an envelope, gave me a kiss on my temple and told me "Happy Sober-thday!" I smiled and lifted my body out of the warmth of the bed. Inside was a letter and an Andean Cross pendant we had purchased the day before.

    As we walked towards the bus, I was able to admire the old, Inca style architecture of Aguas Calientes. The namesake meaning "Hot Water", had natural hot springs at the crown of the small city. It was built on a steep incline, sweeping down the side of cliffs, surrounding a river. *It's hard to explain but worth a quick search online.* Just imagine an old hidden town on the side of a mountain, that has been gentrified to accommodate tourists year-round, eager to visit Machu Picchu. Buzzing like N.Y.C. … but… different in every way. Cafe's, restaurants, gift shops and spas… all alive with native's showing you why you should enter their shop or join them for a meal. Of course at 4:30 in the morning, things were tranquil on those stone streets. Only a few people joined the resident dogs meandering in the early hours. A very different scene from just hours before.

As we descended towards the buses, a line began to form of tired, yet excited travelers. We hunkered down in a spot at the back to wait for the adventure to begin. There were two dogs walking down the line towards us, one very obviously pregnant. They were in an argument; mamma wanted her space from this bigger fur-friend. Back and forth they would growl and nip at each other, stopping right near us. The mamma, noticeably tired, plopped herself down right behind us. Daddy-dog came over and sat cozily right on my feet. My mom thought this was quite profound, that of all the people standing on this line, he came and sat ON MY feet. This was nothing new for this trip as the strays knew who would give them some lovin' if they wanted it. Peru is home to stray dogs everywhere, some of which I had even purchased dog food for in towns prior. This trip only more deeply solidified my loving energy for animals.

We boarded the bus headed for the top of the Inca trail and ascended slowly around sharp curves with steep grades. You'd think the buses were too long to round these curves, but the drivers did their jobs well. Although, I could feel the nerves vibrating throughout the bus at every turn.

I had put together a small box of treasures for this special day. It carried my favorite necklaces, which included a small glass pendant that had the ashes of my dad inside, a beautiful wire wrap with stones that a friend had made, and a pinecone pendant with Labradorite. I also carried a small obsidian horse statue from a spiritual retreat I did during early sobriety. Lastly, a close friend who lives on the beach had always wanted to travel to Machu Picchu, but realized she probably wouldn't in this lifetime. She had given me a shell to place somewhere special in the lost city, almost as if she would leave a piece of herself there, being that she is tied to the sea.

    I could already, deeply, feel that this day would be a special one, remembered for the rest of my life. My excitement grew with each turn towards the top. The parking lots were buzzing with tired, yet wired, tourists and guides. Finding our place in line, I noticed I was still very sleepy...*kind of that weirdly drunken and hazy feeling*... but was quickly distracted from that.

    The sun began to peek over the tops of the skyscraping mountains, sending spectacular rays across the valley towards us. It continued to get stronger and more beautiful as the sun rose and as the line moved us closer to the gates of "archeological site heaven".

    Keep in mind that today was **already** a deeply and emotionally joyous day. When we entered Machu Picchu and scanned the ancient grounds, my mom and I both began to cry. The energy surged through us like a gasping breath of fresh air. The rays from the sun were clear and crisp, divinely casting the spirits of the Inca warriors over their land that once flourished with ritual, prayer and agriculture.

We practically had the place to ourselves in that moment, which made it even more special. After slowly walking across the east side of the grounds, we met a family of resident alpacas waking up for the day to greet us.

The ancient city of Machu Picchu was built in the 15th Century at 8,000 feet elevation! It is surrounded by 2 peaks, one with the city's namesake, Machu Picchu, meaning "Old Mountain". The other peak, Huayna Picchu, means "Young Mountain".

Our mission at hand was to conquer the peak of Young Mountain. The second we saw the mountain, my mom and I looked at each other in shock and said to our guide, "we are supposed to climb to the top of **that**?!" We were amazed at how steep it was, shooting right out of the mountainous ridge. A spectacular sight, indeed!

The ascent to the top of Huayna Picchu was one of the most beautiful hikes I have ever done. Switchbacks meandered up the steep peak, stairwells carved into the rocks escalated us up ridges, vine handrails led us to incredible vistas. The views from our way up the mountain gave a sense of the enormity of the lost city of the Inca people.

They built this whole citadel in less than 50 years and only ruled for about 100 years! They even managed to get a stone structure at the peak of Huayna Picchu to store grains. They would make THIS steep 800-foot hike just for their food! *Imagine the shape they were in!*

It's pretty insane the work that they did throughout the Sacred Valley, with Machu Picchu as the "motherlode" of old architectural cities around the world. Our whole trip consisted of ruin finding, leaving us more in awe with each one we visited. Machu Picchu was definitely the pinnacle of what they call "archeological sites".

Coming up on the peak, we found a spot to have some snacks with an overlook of the city. It was astonishing to us how easily we made it up this steep hike. I could feel the Inca, Warrior, Goddess energy inside me that guided me up this mountainous trek… in a total state of bliss.

I was amazed at how big the lost city of Machu Picchu actually was from looking down upon it…even from far above. The city stretched across the whole ridge.

I did a small meditation with the treasures I had brought with me. As I finished and came back to, I found a small ledge to place my friend's shell, tucked in some moss, protected. I was completely at peace, feeling the magic that ran through the aqueduct veins of the city below. Beautiful little birds, called White-Lined Tanagers, swooped and chirped, dancing through the vast Andes mountains. I could see the rapids of the Urubamba River below, far far below… a tiny vein of a stream in the deep valley. These peaks shot straight at the sky, only something Pacha Mamma could create.

I will never, ever forget that day. The whole trip to Peru still sits with my soul, jolting me with reminders quite often.

I got lost there for a second...What were we even talking about?

Oh yeaaaa, sitting at my house, on lockdown, and with my days... doing nothing and something at the same time.

~*~

We were able to reopen the spa in mid-May, after being closed for 2 full months. There were a lot of changes, new Covid sanitation protocols, schedule staggering for social distancing in the lobby, training and certifications…all on top of a new computer system that was about to be rolling out in all locations nation-wide. *Why they thought now was the time to do that was beyond me.*

The day after we re-opened, a full-blown double rainbow graced us right outside the spa. There were good things to come, but no one knew how quickly or slowly. Those good things couldn't come quick enough…

So one day nearing the end of May, I was sitting at my desk. I can't recall exactly what I was doing. I looked over at Kalypso, and he was bleeding from his face!! He has always had 2 little black dots on either side of his nose. The one on his left side became a mole at an early age, but the vet said not to worry about it...so I didn't.

That mole was bleeding! Heavily!

I washed my hands, grabbed a clean paper towel and rushed back to him. At this point it was bleeding so heavily that it ran down into his nostrils and made him sneeze. Blood was spraying from his nose. I ran to the closet with reckless abandon, grabbed an old sheet and was back to him within seconds. He let me pick him up, set the sheet down, place him down and then proceed to clean his nose. *Mom to the rescue.*

It stopped bleeding for only a moment, or five, and then started back up. I watched him like a hawk the rest of the night. Eventually, it stopped bleeding and I was able to get some sleep. His nose stayed dry for almost a week... and then... started again really badly a couple days later. I called the vet and after speaking with them in a frantic manner, had an appointment booked for a few days away. He would need biopsy and removal, with stitches and the dreaded cone.

Being stupid Covid-times, I couldn't even attend the surgery. Normally, they will at least let you stay in the waiting room! I had to sit at home, try not to bite all my nails off, and wait.

My poor baby came home with 7 stitches in his nose, antibiotics and a cone that he was not happy about. I took it off when we got home, just for a break. He didn't try to mess with it at all, so I left it off and watched him.

All went well and Kalypso got his stitches out 2 weeks later, with no need to wear a cone at all! Turns out the bump on his nose was Hemangiosarcoma, an aggressive tumor of blood vessel cells. They were really happy to be able to get all of it out quickly, as was I. I never thought I would be removing a cancerous tumor off my kitty's face! That **would** happen this year... he's still cute as a button though, maybe cuter. *Pure purrrrfection.*

~*~

The latest news brought terror across the country.

Headlines read: "**Murder Hornets have arrived in the U.S.**"

Are you serious?! As if we weren't dealing with enough, they name these beasts "murder" hornets?! A little extreme, right?

These invasive insects, part of the hornet family, were actually Asian Giant Hornets, native to different tropical parts of Asia. They somehow ended up in Washington, maybe on a flight or cargo shipment...

The country lost their minds with the fear of them spreading. These suckers can grow up to almost 2 inches long, have a wingspan of 3 inches long and are all equipped with a quarter inch stinger. I heard their stings felt like a bullet, and released a potent venom that could kill a human if stung multiple times. *Freaking YIKES!*

The news of these giant psycho-killers came and went, like many things sweeping through the news as of late. No one knew if they were even actually IN the country, because we didn't hear anything past the daunting headline that they had arrived.

Literally the news was flying past us like murder hornets, no one even stopping to fact check or research...*what was next?*

The next event of the year stuck... and is still being talked about, and fought for, to this day... the death of Minneapolis man, George Floyd, at the hands of police force and brutality.

In today's age, everything is recorded. Bystanders videotaped as police officer, Derek Michael Chauvin, cut off George's airways for over 9 minutes with his knee, as he suffocated.

"I can't breathe."

Even witnesses were shouting at the officer to stop. George Floyd was pronounced dead at the hospital. All over a **potentially** fake $20 bill. Because George Floyd is one on a much-too-long list of black persons that had been killed due to police brutality, this event awakened a monster around the country and the world, and the "Black Lives Matter" movement was born.

People were angry, sad and tired that there had been no changes in 2 other long-standing pandemics: racism and police brutality.

Cities began protesting **peacefully**, but when a Covid-induced "safer at home by 10pm" curfew was broken, police security used rubber bullets on a crowd and aggressive riots broke loose in cities all over the **world**.

These were for both Black Lives Matter and fighting, again, against police brutality.

Things were getting bad, but a statement needed to be made. Buildings were being burned and vandalism strikes were happening everywhere. Historical statues were being pulled down if they had anything to do with promoting racism or slavery. This was a REVOLUTION.

We were a little bit scared about what was happening in Denver, especially with Covid still going on. These protests were turning violent, and all creating "super spreader" events of the virus. It was also tying into the pandemic in a way, with protests of mask mandates in general.

"I can't breathe."

Masks were required for the safety of you and those around you, there was no shame in that.

Black lives matter. They always have, and they always will. We have to continue to fight for them and the oppression that still happens in this country. Police brutality in this country and the world MUST stop!

All of this was the movement; personal freedom to choose, equality for everyone and safety from law enforcement. "Protect and Serve vs Harass and Disturb" (That is a quote from a song by the Kottonmouth Kings.)

Only humans can cause this much trouble, I swear!!

So that's it for May. Besides the tangents, can you believe we're only in month **FIVE**?!

~*~

In the beginning of June, my cousin Rikki stopped here in Colorado from Florida on her way to Oregon for an animal rehab internship. Along with her, she brought a **gargantuan** snowstorm. This seemed to be her norm, dubbed the "snow goddess", as she had traveled here the year before and the poor Florida kids had to drive in a blizzard in the middle of the night...in spring! *Colorado at its finest.*

We took a walk in the woods on the trail behind my mom's house and literally, a split second after we walked in the door, the wind kicked up, stronger and stronger, out of nowhere! My mom jumped outside and snatched the hummingbird feeder that was flailing around, sending sugar water everywhere! Later on, we would learn this wind event was called a "Derecho". This weather phenomena will be mentioned again later in this story, unfortunately, a couple different times.

Anyway, the wind howled across the sides of the house, the trees whipped around giving high fives with their crowns. We heard a loud crack, looked behind us, and witnessed a tree fall, thankfully away from the house. The tree did a trust fall, being caught right in the split of another tree that had broken a few weeks before due to high winds.

That tree had been holding a tire swing that my dad had hung when I was 2 years old! My dad Macgyvered that swing into the tree over 28 years ago! He basically cut most of the tread out of a tire, leaving only a seat for my little toddler body. Then hung the rings from rope and viola, a swing!

Many moments had been spent on that swing, many things figured out in my life. *The end of an era*. My mom's yard would never be the same without it, but this year was bringing bigger lessons, to be figured out on a bigger swing.

After the wind died down, we hung the hummingbird feeder back out with a fresh batch of sugar water. It began to snow, big fluffy flakes...in JUNE. Rikki and I sat, watching confused Hummingbirds guzzle down the sugar water. One big guy, we named Bruce, was being very territorial with the feeder. Any time another hummer would attempt a drink, he would lift his plump little body and chase them off. Bruce did not want to share, but little did he know that up on the second level, sat another full sugar water. The other birds got their fill before finding a hidden branch for a nap until summer came back. Bruce napped by his food, tucking his head and needle-sharp beak against his bulging belly. I couldn't take my eyes off of him, his personality was as sharp as his face.

My mom and aunt are both die-hard Springsteen fans, so they were not amused that their daughters named the fat hummingbird Bruce. In my mind, I was thinking of the shark from Finding Nemo, which will always be one of my all time favorite flicks, a classic for my generation. *"Ello, my name is Bruce!"* runs through my head in the heavy Aussie accent, every time.

The snow was gone as quick as it came, classic Colorado weather... never boring. My cousin and I made sure to get a quick snowman built before it melted, with a dandelion for a nose and a flower pot for a hat. A mixture of seasons and nature's elements.

There were little patches of green all around the snow-woman. You could tell it was summer, just taking a quick nap while winter came out... like multiple personalities.

Looking back at pictures you would have thought it was December. We were ready for a hike the next day, a summery walk in the woods.

The hummingbirds were back to normal after their 8-hour hibernation, buzzing and swarming a full canister of freshly brewed sugary goodness, made by yours truly. Bruce was a little bit nicer too, even being plump, the cold made him grouchy.

Before I left to go back to the city, my mom surprised me with an invitation to meet a dog she was thinking about adopting! This was the first time I was hearing about her even thinking about adopting another dog! We had just lost my childhood dog, Blaze, a short three years earlier. That still hurts my heart, but I have never met a dog I didn't like, so I was all in for meeting another one.

Walking up to the foster's apartment, a beautiful black and white dog came barreling towards me. I assumed this was Buddy, our potential adoptee. I guessed right, and boy was he sweet, lush for lovin'. I knew my mom would end up with him, especially after my immediate stamp of approval.

From the moment we met, I could feel Blaze's energy within Buddy. He had the happy demeanor, beautiful Border Collie and Aussie blood (just like my Blaze), and gorgeous black and white coat to match his breed. What caught me the most though, were his calming brown eyes. He looked at me just like Blaze did and my heart thumped in my chest. Catching him laying down, I noticed his paws were crossed. Blaze and Zorro (our other dog and father to Blaze) both loved to lay just like that. *They were there.*

A quick back story on Blaze and Zorro, if you will…

When I was 9 or 10, we wanted to get a family dog. We agreed that the right one would find us, so we waited. One day my mom saw an ad from the shelter for a dog that was found in the next town over.

It was the 4th of July and that town was having a parade, so we went and when the animal shelter truck went by, there he was. His big brown eyes and fiery orange coat drew us in...

Zorro, my first dog, was tucked into one of the gated carriers and had locked eyes with us. He watched us, and he knew... as we watched him, that he was ours. We literally went to the shelter right after the parade and picked him up. We might have even left early, I can't remember anything, only that I was unable to contain my excitement.

A week or so later, my mom took him out to the ranch she worked at, and a woman stopped her.

"Oh my God! Did you adopt this dog?!" My mom replied surprised, "Yea! How do you know Zorro?"

The woman gave her a look, "Well I was the one that brought him to the shelter, and while he was at my house, he got my border collie pregnant! I have 7 puppies at my house!" Needless to say, we ended up with one, Blaze. Zorro and Blaze brought so much joy to our family. They were identical, too! They would never admit it, but between my mom, step-dad and me, I was the only one that could always tell them apart.

Sadly, we lost Zorro a few years later to an accident on a roadway. We had Blaze until he was 15. We lovingly helped him pass when his body and quality of life gave out. Those were two of the hardest moments in my memory, but we don't have to go there. *Why can't our animals live as long as us?!*

The spirit of Blaze ran through Buddy, I could feel it. He was a perfect dog for my mom, sharing that strong rescue-pup energy. His eyes spoke all the gratitude that was possible.

When he arrived in Colorado, he was still healing from a huge gash in his back. Someone had found him in their barn in Oklahoma and nursed him back to health. He's got a pretty badass scar now, but it hides under that thick, black fur. Mountain Pet Rescue helps a lot of dogs from those areas find homes. Then they get to be heavily spoiled, living the fantastic life of a mountain dog.

Somehow, he too, ended up filling an emptiness in our family that only a dog could fill. Just like Zorro, and then Blaze, Buddy too, came to us when and how we least expected. It was better that way.

Who rescued who?

~*~

Amongst all the craziness and new protocols that re-opening the spa brought, corporate decided it was time to plunge into the other daunting task... the change of computer booking and payment systems. Our spa was one of the first to change in the whole nation. Being a nationally recognized chain and us being located smack dab in the middle of the country, we were the guinea pigs! *Great!* It's really not worth it for me to go through all the frustrations with you now, but let me say that I almost quit...a few times!

There were so many new Covid protocols in place including temperature taking, heavy sanitization and disinfection by all personnel, and keeping up with the endless changes regarding safety. On top of that, 30 employees needed to be doing these new requirements on an hourly basis in their massage rooms, along with learning the new system for their client notes and enhancements to services.

Guess who was responsible for keeping ALL of that up to standard...

Imagine the role of the manager at that point; changing the involvement and expectations, training on the new system and hiring new people to replace those we lost during the shutdown!

Welp... that was all me. It almost killed me, but I am proud to have that on my resume now and to have grown from rising to the task at hand. I am no longer employed with the spa, as I had enough by March of 2021. I now happily work from home. *Told you it ruined me!*

~*~

  I'm sure everyone binge watched something over the course of Covid.
  Carter and I watched all the Marvel Universe movies in chronological order. There are like 30 movies...quite the journey. It gave me a whole new appreciation for the comic saga and the huge multi-verse that was created. The movies are, for the most part, gripping... if you like superhero action, or follow the comics. It's not everyone's jam though! When we were done I literally didn't know what to do with myself because I was Marvel crazy. I definitely geeked out on it a little. I even found an extension pack for the card game, Cards Against Humanity… "Avengers Against Humanity". There were some *ridonkulous* cards in there. If you know the game, imagine the crazy things they can make happen with super powers, Thor, Captain Marvel or Spiderman!
  After that I watched Young Sheldon and went right into Big Bang Theory. My aunt had always loved that show. I would see episodes here and there and always thought they were so weird, but that's because I had no connection to it. Watching it from start to finish gave me a true "quarantine crew", because I hung out with them for hours every night. I might mention there are 12 seasons of Big Bang alone!

They fed into my geeky chapter, talking about Marvel, Star Wars, Harry Potter, and other series that we had watched somewhat recently. We had a lot of time on our hands in the weeks between our apartment flood and the move, and then Covid! With the characters of Big Bang, I felt like they were my homies. I laughed out loud, cried, and felt their funny quirks as my own. I was genuinely sad when it was over, and felt like I had said goodbye to a chapter, a group of friends. Then I realllllly didn't know what to do with myself.

If you have not seen Young Sheldon or Big Bang Theory, I highly suggest it for your next binge.

~*~

This point puts us smack dab in the middle of June in our tale, imagine that... halfway through the year. You can't quit now; the second half of 2020 was just as entertaining and menacing as the first.

One of the last days in June was spent playing on the water up in the mountains. Becca and Andrew and their dog, LaLa, were out on their paddle boards. My mom and I decided to blow up her blue ducky, which is mainly used for whitewater rafting. The craft is actually designed for that, but it was the only vessel we had. We had a life-jacket for Buddy so he was able to come with us in the boat. We bribed him aboard with turkey, and once we got him in there, he was extremely calm, much to our surprise!

We paddled around for a while and my mom and I got a good taste of the reason that duckies are made for whitewater, as our rubber boat started to fold beneath us. We weren't sinking or anything, but it made it extremely difficult to keep up with the paddle boards. Nowhere to be... we couldn't help but laugh about it.

As Buddy sat calmly on my mom's lap, she noticed he had a black diamond on his head. Being from a ski town, she started thinking about the black diamond expert runs at Mary Jane Ski Area, a part of the Winter Park Ski Area.

She started thinking about changing his name to one of the ski runs at "The Jane".

Andrew suggested, "How about Outhouse?!" We both looked over at him, like "really"?!

"I am NOT naming my dog Outhouse!" my mom exclaimed. She started running through names of Black Diamond (expert level) runs.

"Boiler, Sleeper, Sterling… Belle Fouche…"

"BUDDY-FOUCHE!" I squealed. It stuck and we all love it. He has since acquired a few other names but he will forever be our Buddy-Fouche… or more recently, Buddy-Fluff-ouche.

My friend Catherine called me up and told me she was fostering two kittens for a shelter and asked if I wanted to come spend some time with them… like it was even a question.

They were only 6 weeks old, something had happened to mamma and they needed newborn care. Tiny little things, taking up only my palm. One was black with bright gray-green eyes, who we called Onyx. The other had a tabby-style striping to her, with blue-gray eyes. We called her Luna. Spending time with them made my heart happy. We got to show them nurturing and motherly care.

A few days later, Catherine called me up in a fret. She explained to me that the vet was warning if Luna didn't gain 3 pounds in 3-4 days, she was going to need heart surgery for a murmur! Being 6 weeks old, they were scared they were going to lose her to the procedure. We spent some time together just sending out good vibes and getting Luna to eat, play and sleep, all on a healthy cycle of loving and careful heart training. This routine ensured the success of her growing-kitten-lifestyle.

We got lucky with this story. Luna made the weight we were hoping for and didn't need to have any surgery! Catherine almost adopted her and Onyx but realized they wouldn't be able to have the best life, since she had 2 big dogs running around. I was so happy to know that Luna and Onyx were on their way to being beautiful, healthy cats suitable for adoption by some lucky kitty parent! We will never know where they ended up, but I know they're being loved fiercely.

On the 3rd of July, news spread of an explosion at a fireworks factory in Turkey! The videos shown looked like a large scale sparkler, which turned the factory to rubble. Apparently it was the 3rd explosion at this site since 2009, which is concerning… but it was prettier than most building explosions, without a doubt!

What newsreel was next?! Keep it coming!

I tell you, 2020 was the year for crazy conspiracy theories and misinformation being sent out into the world like bullets. Some people believed anything and everything they were told!

Right about this time, a documentary came out on Netflix, called <u>Our Social Dilemma.</u> This tied right into what was happening across Social Media in the world, becoming a machine that controls us, with ads and fake news. WE are THEIR product.

There was no credibility for news, meaning anyone could make anything into something resembling real news! You actually had to search for proper sources for the truth. This was a sad awakening. The documentary called out the deep-rooted evil that is Social Media if you are not using it safely and with a "grain-of-salt" attitude.

This monster has and continues to cause widespread depression, inclusivity for some… mild "FOMO" (Fear of Missing Out) for many… and suicide for others… including too many teenagers who felt like they didn't fit into the "world". A sad world, at that.

I could spend pages on this subject, but the sad truth is… you should do the research on your own. Since deleting Facebook from my phone, I felt liberated, more productive, loved by those around me who take time face to face and I sleep better!!

<u>Our Social Dilemma.</u> Check it out.

Within the next year, Facebook and Instagram ended up back on my phone mainly because I couldn't get enough of adorable animal videos. Also, with Covid, I really wanted to be able to keep in touch with my international people.

I think you're ok if you are remaining careful with your content and "likes". What you share can make or break your experience with the platforms... *to each his own*. That's just my two cents...

~*~

One of my best friends from high school, Asa, turned 30 on the 4th of July and had a safe, socially distant-ish party. At this point in time the numbers were going down in "daily Covid cases" so people were loosening up with the mask wearing. As I recall, I was not wearing a mask at his party, but I was doing my best to minimize close contact.

We ate veggies and smoked brisket and chatted around the table, stunned once again at the craziness happening in the world and that Asa was turning 30! He was the first of our crew to hit the big 3-0! My birthday was wild, too… coming up in December, but we'll get there!

We stuffed ourselves, not being able to stop sneaking pieces of brisket from the platter. It was time for the "30" Pinata! Of course, they let the kids swing first. They batted and batted as Asa pulled the string up and down, forcing them to miss, and him to laugh. It was twice as funny because he was half drunk and kind of laughing at himself, too.

Finally, Asa's turn. We made him chug what was left of his beer, spin around a few times and then swing, blindfolded of course! He took one swing and missed but quickly swung again, striking the shimmering 30 shape into 4 pieces. Candy went everywhere, but so did shooters of Fireball and Jack Daniels. Kids dove in for the candy as parents attempted to beat them to the ground for the shots involved. Asa slid in and bounced off his belly, knocking his stepson Niko to the ground. All was well, but my cheekbones hurt from laughing so hard.

Moments later, his lady brought out giant red, white and blue cupcakes. Asa eyed them mischievously as she set them down on the table.

"I want to shove one of those in your face so bad," I said, completely joking.

Asa shrugged, "Only if you videotape it."

"Done!" I handed my phone to Carter and grabbed a cake. In seconds, frosting covered the whole bottom half of his face and squished up into his nostrils. From behind the curtain of frosting, Asa opened his mouth and I shoved the cupcake into his gaping cave, prying the paper away.

Asa got the chocolate cake down and proceeded to farmers-blow the excess frosting onto his lawn. The best part? The frosting dyed his face red and blue. We discovered it was painting anything it landed on. *Sucker!*

Carter and I got home right as the sun was going down, parked on the roof and watched the fireworks start to go off around Denver. We could see all the way from Broncos Stadium and downtown to the southern cities of the front range!

Because of Covid, there was a gathering ban, so no one was allowed to do commercial fireworks that would bring large groups of people together! You'd think this would just be a year for less fireworks, but judging from what we saw, that was definitely not the case!

Nope! Every inch of land that I could see had fireworks beginning to soar, getting smaller and smaller as the landscape regressed. Hundreds and hundreds of fireworks came from every corner of every neighborhood. Everyone had the same idea, private spectacles. People obviously "went north", as the saying goes, which meant to Wyoming. The first exit from Colorado to Wyoming on I25 is a giant strip of fireworks stores, the big ones! I was amazed at how many we saw.... It was truly quite the spectacle!

~*~

In the middle of July, I was invited to a Women's Warrior Goddess retreat up in the mountains. My mom and longtime friend, Brenna, would be in attendance. I really needed to spend some time with both of them! We spent the weekend relaxing, eating good, nutritious food and doing yoga. The leader, we learned, had been carrying a Sage-herb horse with her for 25 years and we were going to burn it at the end of the retreat. She asked us to take anything we wanted to let go of, and put it into the horse. It could take on any fear, heartache, sadness, frustration, sickness, regrets... anything that would be able to burn away with the creature, who was strong enough to take all of that energy in, and carry it for us into another realm and release it.

It was powerful just being in the loving arms of a group of women, vulnerable with the energy we all brought. The conversations ran deep. Creating those connections is what life is about.

Brenna led us in our very own Paint-N'-Sip, but we got to paint whatever we wanted. She just gave us painting pointers, practicing for her art degree she was approaching!

The creative space opened a lighthearted afternoon of munching on fruit, sipping flavorful tea, and being completely raw with our new warrior goddess tribe.

We ended the retreat with a little party, eating all the leftovers from the weekend, which is my kind of party! It was pretty cool being at a "retreat" where I grew up, as it felt like a stay-cation in the mountains! I felt that I was able to release negative energy I had built up over the course of the year, and was supported by others who also carried some unnecessary weight.

~*~

August brought a chapter of fear that none of us expected, some things out of our control as a minuscule species on this earth. Others… preventable.

On August 4th, an explosion happened in the Lebanese capital, Beirut, that looked like an atomic bomb. It first exploded normally (if you will) into a mushroom cloud, and then a huge dome blast that sent a shockwave over the city, killing hundreds and harming thousands more.

We came to learn that this blast was caused by almost 2,800 tons of Ammonium Nitrate, which is normally used as an agricultural fertilizer. The chemical was, most likely stored unsafely and improperly, in a warehouse near the city's port. Just to break this down a little more…2800 tons is 5,600,000 pounds…

This chemical comes in a grainy, salt-like form and when introduced to moisture, forms a solid rock. It was thought that a nearby fire set the chemical ablaze and it basically created a lethal bomb.

An explosion like this creates a high pressure wave, traveling faster than the speed of sound.

It blasted glass right out of windows, literally flipping cars over and sending people flying. The videos were like those out of a war movie, and the explosion was one that only computer-graphic imaging could recreate. *Or you could go watch the video on YouTube...*

This was one of the top 3 largest industrial accidents involving an explosive chemical ever recorded. True 2020 fashion, it hit the city amidst the pandemic and economic crisis, leaving almost 300,000 people homeless in an already dire situation. The hospitals, which were structurally compromised by the blast, were overrun with injured citizens, to join the many coronavirus patients already there.

My heart goes out to those who were affected by the blast. Rewatching the video of the explosion gives me chills, and blows one's mind, just as it did the city.

Oh 2020. What have we done to deserve this?!!

The Williams Fork Fire ignited in the mountains right next to my hometown and it was headed straight towards it. My mom was packing some essentials due to a potential "reverse 911" order, where they tell you to leave... she was basically in pre-evacuation. They wanted everyone to be ready in case the firefighters weren't able to contain it. My mom's house was literally in Pre-Evacuation Zone **ONE**. Her house bordered the town, closest to the burning mountain range. This, obviously, had me in a state of panic and fear. With not being able to get up there to help her from the city, I felt bad making her have to work harder to grab some things from my dad's passing and artwork that I'd made or acquired over the years. Only the top faves come out in those situations, if anything at all.

I watched the fire reports like a job, every move, every update.

Shortly after the news of the fire, another wildfire started near Fort Collins. The Cameron Peak fire was raging through the mountains of the Continental Divide, causing evacuations and already burning many structures, even at its young age.

The sky in Denver began to fill with smoke. Just days into the fires, it felt apocalyptic. The sun was blood red and looked like a 2-D disc from how thick it was covered. You could actually look right at the sun...

When we moved into our apartment, I picked one to face West, to face the mountains. At that point, I felt like I was living in Nebraska or Iowa. The horizon just had no shape. The silhouettes I had always counted on to be there were invisible. I felt lost, on top of being scared to death that my hometown was going to burn to the ground.

The smoke filled the air for days, as both fires continued to grow. The Cameron Peak Fire was now pushing to be the biggest wildfire in Colorado history.

Sadly, as the weeks went on, we were getting used to the sky being red, the sun being clouded and the scent of heavy smoke filling the air. But hey, being COVID times, everyone was prepared with face masks! I shake my head when that becomes a "bright side" type of thought.

Images and time lapses were posted of smoke billowing up from behind the mountains. Wildlife was now coming out into our communities as they had in Australia at the beginning of the year. Folks in the mountains were leaving buckets of water in their yards for the wildlife. We offered them sanctuary in this time of despair. Moose, bear, deer and even a few mountain lions were spotted throughout the outskirts of town!

Of course, a heavy drought accompanied the flames, making the forests in Colorado like a matchbox. Not to mention that over the past decades, Pine Beetle had devastated the forests, leaving trees dried out to their core. This was the best fuel for wildfire. Trees would engulf in flames as if they were soaked in gasoline. That image burned in my brain, pun intended.

In all honesty, the forest needed a big burn, to help clear some of the dead trees. But any fire in Colorado is always too close to home.

~*~

Remember the dreaded windstorms called "Derecho"? Well, one of those angry suckers whipped through the midwest sometime in the middle of August. This thing was no joke, ripping through Iowa and the surrounding states. Carter's parents live in Cedar Rapids, Iowa. Some areas saw 120 mile per hour winds, which is equivalent to a Category 3 Hurricane, sustained for 57 minutes!!!

When they reached out to us after it went through town, they gave us the news. The big, old tree in their backyard had been ripped right out of the ground like a simple weed. The front yard was also home to a big tree that now sat as a broken stump. They were also gifted with a gaping hole in their roof, right in the kitchen, allowing water and branches to move in and seek shelter.

Due to this natural, yet freak, disaster, Cedar Rapids was now missing almost 60% of the city's tree canopy. Giant trees stood cracked in half, like broken toothpicks. Branches flew miles from their home tree, a one-way ticket to the next town over.

The Carter's house project was a big one, and contractors were in short supply since so many homes needed repair. His parents were sad, the big backyard tree had housed cardinals, hawks and other smaller residents. Not to mention also provided shade on their beautiful arbored deck and garden, both of which his father cherished.

His mom was gifted 4 trees from her work, as part of a local program to "rebuild" the canopy. They were to have two of them planted in their yard and donated two to the park behind their house. As weeks went on, they were lucky to get a contractor that re-did their kitchen, flooring and roof in efficient fashion.

Unfortunately, some of Carter's friends were robbed of $3,000! They put a deposit down for their housework and never heard from the guy again! *Some people just suck…*

Again, with that underlying need for money from Covid happening, their story was all too familiar to a lot of residents in the city.

From Iowa to Indiana, there was an estimated $7.5 billion in damage…with millions of acres of crops ripped up. These communities were in for a long road to recovery, joining a club of many around the country with everything going on!

A little bit of lighthearted news came later in August, when Carter and I celebrated our 6-year anniversary. I was working at the spa and shortly before I left for the day, a beautiful "Edible Arrangement" arrived for me. Chocolate strawberries and chocolate covered pineapple filled the bouquet, with honeydew melon and cantaloupe sprinkled throughout. I am not the kind of girl who likes bouquets of flowers really, but give me some fruit, especially covered with chocolate and I am a happy lady!

I can't even remember what we did that night, but I do know that right around that day, we noticed baby habanero peppers on our vertical "Tower Garden". That thing was the closest thing to a growing child we had, besides the kitties of course. I remember exclaiming, "Baby Peppas, babe!" Little did we know that, in the coming months, the damn thing would explode with habanero peppers.

A night in, celebrating our love, our little family, our health and our safety. That's all I could ask for. *Remaining grateful for our blessings was so important, and always will be.*

A short week later, Hurricane Laura ripped through Louisiana and into Texas, making landfall as a Category 4 hurricane just after midnight on August 27th. This was just days after the 15 year anniversary of deadly Hurricane Katrina that rocked the same area. Just for comparison, Katrina made landfall as a Category 3! This storm was a monster off her rocker.

Laura's storm surges accompanied 150 mile per hour winds, ripping up trees and filling their root space with water instantaneously. Some areas saw 19 foot surges of water...which meant water rose up to 20 miles inland. A casino broke loose from its foundation and became wedged underneath Interstate 10 in Lake Charles, LA, which saw the most damage of any city.

Apocalyptic images showed the casino, as well as thick black smoke from a chemical plant fire, foliage, powerlines and housing all strewn about like an angry giant with a wrecking ball had come through.

The winds knocked out power to more than 800,000 homes and businesses in southeast Texas, Louisiana, Arkansas and Mississippi, according to power outage sites. Small tornadoes were even seen in Arkansas and Mississippi from lingering wind speeds.

Windows were shattered, TV towers toppled, roofs shredded, highways drowned, people and animals displaced. Power lines down, along with trees, were blocking roads… this could go on and on… the destruction was widespread and severe.

This hurricane was the strongest on record to ever make landfall in Louisiana, barely surpassing the "Last Island Hurricane" in 1856, measured by maximum sustained wind speeds.

It's crazy to research and learn that Hurricane Laura was created from a large tropical wave off the west coast of Africa, becoming a tropical depression within days and then a deadly hurricane a few days later.

Has anyone heard of the butterfly effect? That's all that goes through my mind. A butterfly flaps its wings on one end of the world and can cause a Tsunami on the other side? Sounds fairly believable now, doesn't it?

Weather can be fascinating, but as time goes on, it seems that it has become more and more intense!! We can't keep up, and we need to do all we can to change this deadly trend.

August. What a doozy! The month brought raging wildfire to the mountains, Category 3 winds through the plains, and a devastating Category 4 hurricane to the south.

Mother Nature is anything but pleased. Can you feel her wrath now?!

~*~

On the first day in September, I went on a hike with my mom, three of her friends (who have also become my friends) and all their dogs. Not having a dog of my own yet, I was in heaven as they all darted around me up the trail!

For most of the day, I led the pack of pups. Buddy was right at my heels, we had become close over the few months my mom had him... love that fluff-fouche! He was followed by Tucker, Maggie's little mutt pup who wore a bell, and her other dog Brooke, a huge, midnight-black, husky and wolf dog mix. Alongside them was Juniper, one of my favorite dogs ever. MJ, her human, has always had Bernese Mountain Dogs, but June-Bug was the best. Her expressive brown eyes often caught the sun and would shoot golden-brown rays of love straight into my heart.

We climbed and climbed, crossing over rippling creeks running through wrinkles in the mountainside. Swaying patches of wildflowers engulfed us standing almost as tall as me! The dogs frolicked over glacial ice. All, except Juniper, did a Polar-Bear-Plunge into the melted water below. We stopped by a small river and pulled out all of our hiking snackies. Veggie wraps, apples, clementine's and who-could-forget the GORP, or trail-mix for those of you who aren't aware of the term. I'm not even sure where that word came from, but it always warrants a giggle on hiking days. *Gorp!*

My mom and MJ told us a story of when they were hiking in this same area some years ago. They were glasading down a snowfield, which basically means trying to ski in hiking boots, when my mom slipped and started sliding uncontrollably down. MJ was able to grab my mom and tried to plant her feet to help stop her. Hand in hand, they both slid down the mountainside on the snow, and just like in a bad dream, there were rocks at the bottom of the snow field. Thankfully, MJ's husband grabbed her arm right before they hit the rocks, a truly incredible save, and very likely lifesaving!

Almost as if Juniper knew I was scared of the story that was being told, her nose came right through my underarm and she gave me a kiss on my cheek.

"Hey pretty lady! Are you having fun?" I rattled behind her ears, kissed her nose and jumped up with her. Junebug's big head shook and she happily followed me downstream.

An energy surged through me, reminding me of climbing Huayna Picchu in Peru. It must be trees and crisp mountain wind that breathes life into me.

We were so close to the top. I started to see peaks of other mountains literally "peek" from behind the horizon and had to keep going.

Walking up onto the summit, the entire valley opened up as the Continental Divide cupped my little hometown in its strong hands. Rugged mountaintops ran for miles, some parts covered with clouds that looked like knitted blankets, exposing the softer side of these immense beauties.

There are a few moments in my life that I have found myself in total bliss, engulfed in gratitude. This was one of those moments. I felt so small but so nurtured, surrounded by Mother Earth at her finest, as she embraced me.

Not a week later, another Derecho ripped through the valley. Earlier in this book, I mentioned the Derecho that blew over my tire swing tree and the one that ripped off the roof of the Carter house in Iowa. This one was angrier. It came from the East, building over the great plains and hurdling over the mountains, which I believe may have slowed it down just enough. Locals talked about it like a mountainous hurricane, with trees and branches whipping across main street with a vengeance. Trees were blown over on either side of the valley, looking like a tornado went through town, thankfully minus houses being lifted.

At the end of the month, I drove up there from the city. Certain runs of trees stood huddled over, crowns hanging from the winds that occurred. Little did I know, they were far from alone.

The next day we hiked up the Jim Creek Trail by the ski resort. Buddy, Brooke and Tucker zoomed around us again which made me happy. It was a cool, fall day in Winter Park.

We got lucky in that our last couple hikes weren't too smoky, since the fire near my mom's was still burning. Thankfully it wasn't as much of an emergency anymore because the fire department in the mountains kicked ass, with this fire and past. We probably wouldn't be here without them.

Moving further up the mountain, we started having to maneuver around trees and stumps strewn across the trail. A logging team had come through with chainsaws and cleared the hiking path, since it was along one of the main water pipes to the city and was a popular local hike.

As we got up to where the trees opened up, I looked around. A 360° view left my jaw on the ground. All of the trees were hunched over towards the West. The best way to explain it would be if all of the trees were standing up straight, and someone came and swept their arm across the top, creating a wave of curved trees. I was shocked that the wind had initiated this destruction. The trail got more impassable as we ascended, so we were forced to stop and turn around about 1/3 of a mile from our destination waterfall.

We left that hike feeling sad and conquered and as if we had just walked through the Apocalypse!! As you have read, the Derechos had wreaked havoc on this country over the summer. Between the fires, wind, other cold, hard evidence of Mother Nature's power and revenge, and the relentless pandemic, it left us feeling extremely defeated.

Well, friends, we are making our way through the year quite nicely. Wouldn't you say? Buckle up, this story isn't over yet.

This last quarter began with me finding out that one of my best friends from high school, ironically also named Carter, was robbed at gunpoint just blocks from his home in the city. My friends and I are hippies; chill, mountain kids. We always felt safe there! Maybe it instilled just a tad too much trust in us...

He was stopped by a small guy, thought to be a teenager, who demanded his wallet and phone. It's one of those true-life moments that makes you center at "Life is more important than anything material." My heart sank with the story, but I was just so happy that my buddy was alive and not too traumatized!

Hug your loved ones, right now if you can. I suggest you hit up a friend and let them know you love and appreciate them and that life is precious. Here, go ahead, I'll give you a moment.

...

~*~

Just a couple days into October, some friends of ours/old roommates got to play a show! Remember the music scene? Colorado was sure trying to make something happen for us music lovers.

We walked into the venue with masks on, and were guided to the table we were assigned. They informed us that we had to stay at our table and could not stand or dance. *What the hell? Was THIS how it was going to be?* I was thinking I would hold off on another show for a while, but who knew how long that would be. It was the weirdest thing, waving to our friends across the "no-dance" floor.

We watched their set, proud that they had this opportunity. In all honesty, an uncomfortable feeling sat in my stomach. It wasn't the too-sweet Shirly Temple I was drinking, but rather the shooters and lines of coke the girls in front of us were doing... not carefully I might add. One girl would pull her mask down, snort a line right off the table and then roll her head around and sway in her chair. By the end of the night they were swinging their masks around like cowgirls with lassos.

Being sober was one thing, but they were more-along-the-lines of "partying like pre-covid". This felt like dirty club vibes. I couldn't escape the way I felt about their actions. It all felt very unsafe, and disrespectful for those trying to stay safe and comfortable at the event.

At that moment, I realized how much of a full-blown-rager every single show would be, once they came back in full swing. The drugs would flow like "Fear and Loathing". It scared my sober ass. Yet, I think I could get used to the whole distanced seating thing in venues that would usually be packed shoulder to shoulder. That's me looking at the bright side with my sober-social-anxiety.

The show was 2 separate sets, the early "chill vibe" show and the late night "down & dirty" set. I think the girls in front of us went to the wrong one...*by accident? I'll never know.* We attended the first and were able to give a quick hug to a couple friends before we left the venue, but were quickly shoo'ed out by the bouncer. Yep, Covid times... 6 feet apart people! *How could we forget?!*

Days later, I found myself fighting tooth-and-nail in a town hall meeting for my hometown. They were proposing building a development partially on a protected wetland. Part of that blueprint was a shooting range, and it would be surrounded by time-share cabins. We could see it, the greedy developers not giving a second thought about our precious mountain lands.

A shooting range in the valley would absolutely destroy the ecosystem in the area with just the sound pollution alone: scaring off birds and native wildlife species. The buildings would destroy a wetland that was protected by a "golden" bill written decades earlier, specifically to protect that part of the Fraser valley. How could anyone be so evil as to rip apart something so sacred, so beautiful. I felt that there was no other way, but to fight.

I am incredibly happy to say that we won that fight, a victory for the creatures that inhabit that land. Later on, they would propose a new blueprint, with much less invasive structures and no shooting range. We would cross that bridge when it came, but my heart was filled with joy about helping protect the valley I will ALWAYS call home.

Touching back on the fires that were still burning and creeping closer to town. The Williams Fork fire, thankfully, was at a higher percentage of containment. The Cameron Peak fire had surpassed the record, and taken the title, of the largest wildfire in Colorado history at over 200,000 acres burned.

On a smoky evening, news came out of another fire that had ignited. It was just west of the town I went to highschool in. Dubbed the East Troublesome Fire, we had no idea how much it would live up to its name. At first, it creeped East, towards town. The fire department had a close eye on this one, by the grace of a higher power making more manpower available due to containment of the Williams Fork fire.

Over the course of the next 24 hours, it engulfed over 100,000 acres of land, passing just North of town. Unfortunately, it was headed towards the beautiful hidden gem of Grand Lake, an old-western town sitting beside the largest natural lake in Colorado and the very start of the mighty Colorado River. Old wooden buildings and a boardwalk make up the one-of-a-kind, tiny town. There's a lot of history there, and this fire was surely becoming troublesome, and worrisome as it barrelled right there.

One of my first jobs was at a marina there, and those memories came emotionally flooding back to me as the East Troublesome became much too close for comfort.

An old coworker had just spent 2 years building a beautiful log home for his family, only to be engulfed in flames only 90 days after its completion. He had only minutes to gather his little one, the 2 dogs and only their most important possessions, before having to race away.

The thought of watching your beloved home be eaten alive by fire in your rearview mirror is heart wrenching. His story was familiar to many, including a friend whose in-laws lost their cabin, boats, snowmobiles, and other prized possessions. The memories from inside those homes, however, can live on.

Skeletons of houses were left behind, oftentimes only chimney stacks remaining as headstones. It was moving too quickly to stop, right towards town. My eyes were glued to the news about it, my heart cracking minute by minute… burning in my chest, so to speak.

Security cameras streamed trees going up like matchsticks, flames barreling closer to the house, and then footage was cut off, charred with blazing heat.

A silver lining here is that only 2 people lost their lives. An old couple, who moved to Grand Lake after their honeymoon decades ago, falling in love with the town the moment they arrived. They chose to stay together, in the home they had created their lives in. Even as their kids asked them to leave for their safety, they held each other tight and went down with the ship, in a sense.

Rest in Peace Mr. and Mrs. Hileman. May your spirits soar among the ashes that will be the rebirth of the forest.

Somehow, by the grace of God, the town of Grand Lake was spared, but many lost their homes to the inferno. It was beautiful seeing the county come together, holding fundraisers, food drives and housing those who had lost their homes or had been evacuated. Small towns have that magic, true neighborly love. My mom even got to house one of her favorite local musicians, along with her husband and dog, and was grateful for having been able to give back and create a deeper friendship with them. *Small town living for the win.*

Within the course of mere hours, due to hellacious winds, the East Troublesome fire doubled in size and became the second largest wildfire in Colorado history, next to the Cameron Peak fire that was still ablaze! It whirled over the mountains and down closer to Estes Park, causing evacuation of many of the neighborhoods there. Elk, moose, bears and other critters were seen scattering through town for their lives. The images were all hazy due to the heavy smoke, almost bringing my head and heart back to the images I saw at the beginning of the year in Australia. *Mother Nature... fighting back... sense a theme happening here?*

Not long after these monsters ripped apart the forests, a news headline warned that the two fires could **merge**! *Like I have said many times, in true 2020 fashion.*

Thankfully they did not come together, due to a divinely intervened snowstorm that helped to contain the fires and inhibit their meeting. Just the fact that they might have met and potentially could have taken Colorado off the map, was enough to blow everyone's mind and stir up a deep doomsday- level-fear. *Someone above, or maybe an army of angels, was watching out for us, no doubt.*

~*~

In November, big wig scientists Pfizer and BioNTech announced that a Covid vaccine was on the horizon. There were now over 230,000 deaths in the U.S. and more than 9 million cases, so it couldn't come soon enough.

Those numbers were rising as people went out to vote in the presidential election, which was probably the most important one ever.

It was just crazy watching the toll numbers roll in, to find out that our country was divided almost perfectly in half. With votes still being counted days after the election, Trump and his team attempted to overturn the election results by claiming widespread voter fraud. There was talk of conspiracy on the Republican side that mail in ballots were being tampered with. Anger flooding from both parties caused a grueling election. Officials in each of the 50 states declared, after some investigation, that there was no evidence of mail-in ballot fraud.

Joe Biden won, after a long fight against the other party and overcoming their attempts to roadblock the transition of power. Trump repeatedly said over the last month of the year that he "would never concede the election".

Only after an anger fueled mob of Trump supporters violently invaded and ransacked the Capitol, did he accept the loss... I'll explain more about this later, but it was all pretty painstaking to watch.

I normally run the other direction when it comes to politics, but this shit was juicy to keep up with. Flabbergasted at my country, I realized why I often keep to myself and enjoy the little things.

I didn't know what I would have done had the Republican party won again, but thankfully I did not have to think about it...this was the first election since 1992 that the president hadn't been reelected... thank whatever higher power there is! The world would not have been able to withstand such a tyrant for 4 more years. Rumors have since spread that he would run again in 2024... Lord help us. *Iceland anyone? Norway?*

For Thanksgiving, we were thinking about getting together with family... but all decided that it would be best to wait. *Stupid Covid. Were we ever going to be in the clear from this thing?*

There was a restaurant that we liked going to and we saw that they were doing take-out Turkey dinner meals. We decided to pre-order one of those and my mom and Buddy came down to the city! I was shocked, thinking it would be a simple, fairly bland meal. The flavors were good, we had tons of leftovers and it felt like a true thanksgiving! Sadly, I would go to order food there in 2021 to find out that the cafe didn't make it through the financial burden of Covid. That went for my other favorite spot in Denver too, Racine's, which had been a Denver staple for decades! We started to see that with all kinds of businesses, restaurants, head shops and mom-and-pop shops. The big wigs of everything were, of course, thriving.

The ripple effects were running deep, and would continue to do so in all industries throughout 2021… and beyond.

~*~

Can you believe we're in December?

My homegrown habaneros had taken over the Tower Garden and it was time to harvest. I decided I could "kill 2 birds with one stone" and that the best way to use all of them up and give presents for the holiday was to make spicy honey! I purchased 3 big jars of local honey, cut up only a fraction of the peppers and infused the two. When I say fraction, I really mean it. I cut up maybe 20 peppers, give or take… and still had… at least another 70 peppers!! We ended up giving friends some of the peppers as gifts too.

I am so grateful that I had some gloves to use, because my hands burned even with the gloves on. I mixed and stirred and whipped and churned… really getting those spicy flakes drenched in sweet sweet honey.

After 48 hours of infusion and constant manipulation, I filled 30 little 1 ounce glass jars of my hot-sticky goodness. The jars I ordered came with adorable little labels that I filled out in excitement: "Watch your mouth! X-mas 2020".

Over the course of the next few months, I would hand them out to anyone that was brave enough to take one. Their feedback was all the same, "Holy shit, that is some spicy honey!"

The craziness continues, I don't know if I'll be able to stop the story at New Years! My birthday was smack-dab in the middle of the month.

Remember earlier in the story I mentioned my birthday was crazy? Well... I was totally joking. Carter and I went to the store and bought all the fixings for a monumental Charcuterie board, garlic shrimp tacos and mocktails. My mom joined us for the evening too. We had to do something for my 30th... even if it was sitting at home. I did get a wonderful birthday present though, a snowstorm! Being a mountain girl, that was always one of the best gifts... especially when it happened in the city... which nowadays, is few and far between.

Two days later, I woke up to completely stiff and swollen hands. My joints felt hot and bulgy for the first hour I was awake. It literally came out of nowhere. It was like that every day for a week, when I realized I probably needed to see a Rheumatologist. That came with its own challenges. A referral was necessary for specialty doctors so I had to book a Primary Care visit first. That was a 3 week wait in itself!

After rounds of doctor visits, blood work and x-rays, I got the diagnosis. Happy 30th to me, inflammatory arthritis. *You'd think I turned 60... that's how I felt anyway.*

Along with that, came a positive blood test result of Hashimoto's Thyroiditis, basically chronic inflammation of the thyroid and an autoimmune disorder that attacks the gland. I knew I was Hypothyroid, but was misdiagnosed years earlier, which is common for Hashimoto's.

I suddenly found myself having to make a 180 degree turnaround, and cut all the good foods out of my diet. I normally eat pretty healthy, but when you are forbidden all the good stuff, you want it that much more. Like I mentioned earlier, during the apocalyptic shopping in early Covid, I was once again grateful for my love of fruits and veggies. *Oh, human nature. Why did I all of a sudden want mac-n-cheese and pizza more than anything?!*

Christmas was a different feeling this year. My family doesn't usually do big holidays, but I usually went to see my mom. We would get up early and exchange gifts over casual breakfast, and then go skiing. This year my mom bought me an IKON ski pass for my birthday/Christmas, before Covid hit.

Because of my hands being inflamed and the pandemic, I decided to defer it to the next season, which was a very nice option that wasn't offered in pre-covid years. It was weird not skiing. I had come to love it, after snowboarding for so long. My life from 2 to 7 years old was on sticks, but when I decided I wanted to try being cool, I dropped skiing and hopped on a board.

Being on a snowboard was thrilling, and I was in with the cool kids. However, once I decided that I would rather have fun and be comfortable, I switched back to skis, when I was 25! Boarding made my body hurt after 18 years, I was aware that I wasn't getting any better at it... and that I was still always afraid that I would catch an edge and break my face!

    I once read in Skateboarding Magazine, also during my "cool kid" phase, a quote. It read "you may fall, but whatever you do, protect your face...for obvious reasons."

    Well said. I have, ever since. I'm a pretty cautious person... never even broken a bone. *Watch, it will happen right after this thing goes public...Better knock on wood.*

    I woke up in my house in the city, turned on our little Christmas tree and called my mom as she was heading out the door to ski. As I looked out the window, I could see a big gray cloud over the mountains and knew right away the fun she was going to have in the new snow. A pout crept across my face, but I wished her a beautiful day, sent my love and let her go have some fun.

    Astounded that it was already the end of December again, I sat and reminisced about last Christmas, since this year would never even come close to the joy from the 2019 Holidays.

    The year before, when all was normal, Carter's parents came to visit from Iowa and rented a gangster Airb-n-b right down the road from our apartment. We got up early and brought over what-felt-like half of our kitchen, to the rental.

As we stepped out of the elevator, I suddenly felt "Hollywood" as it opened up directly into the apartment! Classy!! I almost dropped the bag I was carrying, in utter star-struck... *MTV Cribs!*

We made a second trip back to the house to collect all the food, and felt like we were moving. I even made a list to make sure everything we were bringing made it home! There was no other way since we were originally supposed to host and said we'd cover most of the sides; all of our pans, pots and strainers were needed.

Carter and I whipped up the green bean casserole, garlic potatoes smashed to silky smoothness, brussel sprouts and chocolate cake for dessert, decorated in a true ugly-sweater look! The red and green frosting got away from me a little...and so did the sprinkles. *Meh, it's a celebration... and it made for a good laugh.*

Views of the mountains and the decorated city kept my eyes wandering all day. The place had a huge, open floor plan. Windows lined every wall, with perfect sitting space in the sills, letting in natural light from all directions. I spent many moments sitting in them, channeling my inner cat. Time well spent, admiring the city light up as the sun went down and catching the picturesque sunset over the Rocky Mountains. All felt right.

The kitchen was something we only dreamed of having. A big island with a sink and a mini fridge, a commercial kitchen fridge and freezer, a 6-top stove, 2 stacked ovens, and plenty of counter space with an extra sink and fancy dishwasher. *Kitchen goals.*

We played games all day as we cooked, sat and ate too many chocolates with Grandpa Gene, admired all the views and walked to the capital to see it lit up after dinner. Having my mom, Carter and his brother and parents, his aunt and uncle, and grandpa all together was truly one of the most joy filled days I've had, one that I will carry with me. Especially now, having lost Grandpa Gene, my giggles return as I remember sneaking chocolates with him before dinner. We knew our appetite couldn't be ruined by anything, especially too many Lindberg chocolates. A truly spectacular holiday and a cherished Christmas memory.

I found myself smiling and borderline drooling, remembering the day. As I came back to the present moment, I realized it was lightly snowing. Honestly, the rest of the holiday is fuzzy, I think Carter and I just ordered food from somewhere and chilled on the couch. I remember wanting to watch The Grinch with Jim Carrey, but might have passed out from a food coma. These last couple weeks of 2020 seemed boring, which was gladly accepted after the rest of the shit that happened over the year.

There were still arguments going on about the election, which I blocked out. *Get this shit over with already, Biden won... can we just focus on getting life back to some semblance of normalcy?*

People were spicy over the holidays at the spa. I realize I haven't mentioned much about my place of employment over the last few months, but there was really a lot of unnecessary drama the whole time. Not even worth going into.

Wahoo… I was in bed before midnight on New Years and fell asleep listening to fireworks rather than watching them. I gladly closed my eyes on the year, with high hopes for 2021, as I imagined the rest of the world did as well….

~*~The Beginning of The End-ish~*~

It seemed like a disservice to end this story with me going to bed before midnight on New Years. There were so many things that happened in 2021 that need to be documented. You should be prepared to drop your jaw just a few more times.

Only 6 days into the year, there was a rally wherein Trump continued his claim that the election was stolen from him. He told the crowd of his unmasked supporters to "never give up, never concede" and told them "to never forget this day". He posted to Twitter, which if you don't recall, he was infamous for... and his continued relentless and inflammatory posts led to his account being locked!

How freaking childish, this guy was supposed to be a leader, and an adult. I couldn't help but laugh at how preposterous all of this was. *Twitter had to block the President!*

Later in the day, after Trump's call to arms, extremists stormed into the Capitol building, breaking windows and glass in doors. The fear of the senators was apparent as they hid for their lives under desks throughout the building. Rioters smashed through the hallways and conference rooms, waving flags and yelling obscenities.

The best part? The rioters were filming everything on their cell phones, many of which recorded incriminating footage that would later be used to convict them! *Palm to forehead...*

Rumors spewed that security and police force on site opened some of the storm gates and allowed people to enter with anger. Footage was later released that showed otherwise, as they begged for backup. Trump, of course, took no blame, and basically told these people to go for it.

I was so grateful that the 4 year wrath of this guy was about to be over. We all hoped for the Biden administration to bring hope and peace back to the divided country. Of course there would be controversy over that administration as well... *will we ever be able to be united fully?*

Enough about politics... my least favorite thing ever.

Can you tell?

...It can be damn juicy though!

Just like my first half of this story, bits of happiness will be sprinkled through this grim epilog.

I got a late birthday present from my friend, Catherine. She came to the spa and we took a walk on my break. She told me to come to her car and handed me some sort of picture wrapped in bubble wrap and tissue paper. When I opened it, tears came to my eyes as I looked down upon a painting of my dear kitty, Kalyspo. It was like a realistic portrait, even capturing the depth of his blue eyes. Now I get to look at him even when he wants to be a typical cat and be alone.

What a gift, one that I'll surely cherish forever! Catherine and I met outside an art class in college. We instantly clicked, figuring out that we had mutual friends and common interests. She stakes a claim to my heart to this day and will forever be my animal hero and giver of the best gifts. *I am going to find her a gift of that epic proportion, one day!*

~*~

In February, the United States reached a grim milestone of 500,000 deaths from Covid-19 and news of a variant was starting to spread, *Delta*. This strain was said to cause major infections and was found to be 2x as contagious as the previous strain.

This seemed like a losing battle.

Thankfully there was now a vaccine available, which was coming in waves and available only to older folks and people with health issues or compromised immune systems at first. It gradually went to younger age groups as time went on. The CDC and World Health Organization were urging folks to get the vaccine, as it was the best defense against the virus, and would help fight it if contracted. Of course, people were leary... this was a brand new virus, brand new vaccine... we didn't know anything about either. This erupted into a huge debate across the country, right on par with what now had become the "Divided States of America". But we don't have to go down that road, for as you can imagine, nothing good can come from going down that rabbit hole. *Is a peaceful agreement to disagree totally off the table, ever?!*

~*~

  Over the course of the years 2019 and 2020, I was taking classes for a certification in Addiction Counseling. Ever since my trip to Peru, I knew I wanted to be in that field. I finished my last class in March of 2020. I had actually set up my computer the day after we moved from the flood because I had a final due. There was way too much going on in the story way back then, so now is a more appropriate time to mention it. Anyway, I had been starting to search for jobs in the field of addiction recovery. Nothing was really coming up that fit my interest or skill set, but I knew it would come in time. Keyword searches on job boards included sobriety, recovery, addiction, addiction recovery. You get the idea.

  In January of 2021, I found an outpatient recovery program that offered a remote position helping with intakes and scheduling for new members looking for help with substance and alcohol use. Did I mention it was *Work From Home*?! Remember how I said working from home ruined me? THIS WAS PERFECT!!! I had applied, and by the grace of a higher power, was selected for an interview. Meant to be.

  In the first days of February, after an intensive interview process, they offered me a position on weekends. I accepted without hesitation. The owner of the spa had known I was looking for something like this, and was very gracious and understanding knowing that accepting this position could change my standing as general manager at the spa. When I told her I had accepted, I gave her a 4 week notice as the general manager and told her that I would still like to work for her in a different capacity.

My start date for the recovery program was the middle of March. I had requested some time off in the beginning of March to go to Iowa with Carter to see his parents and it all was falling into place nicely, time-wise. My plan was to be "demoted" from manager at the end of February, and come back in March as a normal ol' spa associate. Fine by me!

My boss seemed excited for me, maybe a little too nonchalant about the fact I was giving notice, after being there for 4 years. Something wasn't sitting right, but I was too excited to spend too much energy on it.

On the last day in February, I had a meeting with her, to discuss what we were doing for promotions in March… or so I thought. When we sat in the office, she proceeded to tell me that she sold the spa… and the new owners were taking over… TOMORROW!!! *Uhhhhh what? Thanks for the notice?!?!*

She scheduled an impromptu virtual all staff meeting for that evening, which we usually would give AT LEAST 3 weeks notice for. Less than half the staff showed up, and upon the news being shared, there was just silence across the computer screen. We were all stunned.

On March 1st, the new owner came and spent the day at the spa. I figured my boss would have mentioned something to her about my resignation as general manager... nope! I had to give notice all over again. And might I mention, this landed on the day after my last 4 week notice had ended.

I told her I had resigned as the GM and was about to be taking a week off to go to Iowa. The time had already been approved by the old owner, flights bought and bags packed. Especially after this bomb was dropped, I didn't owe this lady anything, neither of them actually. I had put my heart and soul into the spa, just to receive this punch in the gut by the boss that I had trusted.

To wrap up this vent-fest... I told her I would stay on for the next 4 weeks but only if it worked with my schedule with the new job and training.

Right as this was all happening, my job offered me a full time position. *How freaking divinely serendipitous was that?!* I managed to make it to the first weekend in April at the spa, working 7 days a week. From what I heard from my past employees who remained there, things got really bad after I left. Good bye and good riddance; what a nightmare!!

I was so grateful to be starting a job that allowed me to work safely from home, with my kitty, and be helping those affected by addiction.

Someone upstairs has my back, I tell you what!

On our vacation in Iowa, I spent the week spoiling Domino, the giant housecat, and playing housewife. Carter and his dad were working on building stairs down from their deck to the backyard. I would come out with lemonade and apple slices, sweat rags and necessary provisions. My mom had flown out there with me and spent a few days with us. We sat down after dinners and played games like Quiddler and Bananagrams, had hours of good conversations and sunset walks in the park.

The last night my mom was there, we had smoked ribs for hours and when we all sat down for dinner, I started to make a toast.
"Wait! I don't have water!" Carter jumped up and filled his glass.
I spoke something along the lines of, "I am so grateful to be here with all of you. They say the best way to a woman's heart is through her stomach. So Carter," I turned to him and grabbed the ring I had brought, "would you do that for me forever?" I couldn't compose myself and was crying by the time I asked because I was so nervous.
He, through blubbery eyes and flushed cheeks, said "Yes! A million times yes!!!"
"It's a damn good thing you grabbed water, Carter!" His dad joked.

Boom, I was locked into a full stomach for life! Becca had been the one to propose to her hubby, so I figured, what the heck, why not, right? Girl power! It took some months before Carter had realized what I had asked of him, and I had to explain it was in fact, a proposal.

One of the more amusing stories of 2021 happened in late March as one of the biggest shipping barges ever built, named the Ever Given, was blown sideways in the Suez Canal in Cairo, Egypt. I need to mention that it is one of the busiest trade routes in the **world**. Winds at 40 knots, about 45mph, blew in, causing the massive vessel to run aground from inability to steer.

The 1,300 foot long barge was wedged sideways, taking up the entire width of the canal, blocking any traffic from getting through. This greatly impacted Asia, Europe and the Middle East. More than 350 ships were waiting to get past the barge, preventing an estimated $9 billion worth of trade from passing through.

I can't really recall if we saw any major impacts from that here in the USA, but it was quite entertaining to witness, being someone who takes interest in seafaring vessels.

~*~

In April I got to go see my family in Florida. It seemed like there was a small window of opportunity that I had to take. Having not seen them since 2019, the window opened and I had to jump through. Being at my aunt's house was so great; just relaxing, swimming, and lounging in the sun. She's got the best set up in her yard. A tiki lounge, complete with games and fun nautical decorations, a sandy beach with a fire pit and a hammock, a giant rock style waterslide into the pool, hula hoops, bikes and a tiki bar to match the vibe. I spend my entire trip out there when I go, who wouldn't?!

My cousin Oliver had a pretty silvery goldfish named Big-Man, who sadly, just sat in an undecorated bowl in the guest room I was staying in. Being the animal lover that I am, I had no choice but to do something about this. Before he knew it I was off to the pet store. I found a little bit bigger tank, got some fun, colorful tiki decorations and purchased another goldfish. He was white, orange and black and looked like confetti, so I named him Buku. A party name fit the bill.

I set up the tank in the living room, placed in all the decorations, turned on the color-changing lights and introduced the fish. Big-Man already seemed happier as Buku swam around him in the colorful tank. All animals deserve a happy life, no matter how big or small.

The day before I left I impulsively scheduled a tattoo appointment and went and got some ink. A small nautical-tribal turtle now lives on my left foot. Many of my tattoos are something I had wanted for a while, but then had gotten inked at some totally random moment. Another "window of opportunity" type thing.

A quick trip, but needed. I came home sun kissed and fulfilled.

I got the first dose of my Covid vaccine on April 18th! Luckily, no side effects followed. I was so grateful as I had known so many people who had suffered a Covid-like sickness after theirs. I have to admit I did feel a small sense of an extra layer of protection...

The world was flabbergasted that this thing was still happening over a year later. Many went back to doing things they wanted to do, like travel. Whether it felt safe or not!

Earlier in the story, I mentioned the conviction of Derek Chauvin for the killing of George Floyd. On April 20th, he was sentenced to 22.5 years in prison for 2nd degree unintentional murder, 3rd degree murder and 2nd degree manslaughter. The world celebrated that day, as this felt like a victory in a world of injustices.

Alright, something happy...

On May 17th, I celebrated another year around the sun without alcohol in my life or my body. My mom and I decided to take a small trip over the mountains to Steamboat Springs. We packed up the Subaru with road trip snacks and Buddy, put on some good tunes and began a weekend of vacation.

Ironically, the cheapest Airbnb available was to rent a room in a house called "Casa Hora Feliz", which means *Happy Hour House* in Spanish. Donna, the owner, instantly invited us for pizza and wine that evening, to which we comically told her the story of being there to celebrate my sobriety but thought her place looked better than any hotel, with the price being right too. She totally understood and told us we could still come for pizza.

We spent the weekend mostly hiking and finding good eats where we could enjoy the patio with the pup. We sat by the river, journeyed to a beautiful waterfall and went to Strawberry Hot Springs. The weekend was perfect and relaxing. Sobriety allows time and energy for self care, whatever that looks like for you. It comes with gratitude and serenity, even in the smallest of forms. Life is brighter, more joyous moments, trials of course, but the good far outways the bad.

~*~

The week after that trip, I went to visit my friend near Tampa, Florida. I was able to bring my work setup with me and get a schedule figured out that would allow us to have some serious fun. I had a beautiful view of the ocean from my makeshift desk. Lucky doesn't even begin to describe my feelings. Remote work for the win!

This was the dear friend who gave me the shell to place at Machu Picchu, Captain Pam!

We went to the Clearwater Marine Aquarium to visit Winter, the dolphin, who starred in the movie Dolphin Tale. They had an exhibit going on about whales, which led us to a virtual reality deep dive with Humpback Whales. It had those fluidly moving seats and everything! We were the only ones in the ride, which was a good thing because we were hooting and hollering. I could hear the workers giggling at us. That was Pam and I though… always chasing the next giggle.

Every evening we walked the 300 yards from her beach cottage to the silky sands of Indian Rocks Beach to watch the sunset. Being that it was turtle nesting season, and the animal fanatics that we are, we got to play King Kong on some sandcastles.

***Teachable moment**…anything that obstructs the turtles path to the nesting site can be fatal for them either coming ashore or returning to the sea after nesting.

ALWAYS make sure that if you are somewhere that sea turtles nest, you kindly destroy your sand creations for the turtles' sake. Also, just for the heck of saying it - pick up your dang trash! *You'd think everyone would know this by now, but we picked up plastic sand toys, bottles, goggles and beach chairs... Help Our Mother Earth!!!*

Anyway, one day we went to Busch Gardens for some thrills. The last time we had gone there together, we regretted not taking the safari and feeding the giraffes. I was hesitant at first because I really despise the way most zoos keep their animals, but Busch Gardens does it right. No cages between the herbivores, they get to free roam in a massive space as they would in wild Africa. They have shade, clean water and health checks!

We hopped up in the back of the truck and held on tight through the rough patches. As soon as the giraffes saw the truck driving up, they made a B-Line for us. I held up the large leafy greens and let them wrap their crazy tongues around them, gently pulling them from my hand. Being that close to such a majestic animal like that had me elated. I didn't want it to end, but the memory lives on as one of the greats! The day ended with a ride on a coaster. Pam forgot to take her phone out of her pocket and at the end of the ride, what do you know...it was gone. When we got back to her house, she pulled up her FindMyPhone on her iPad and we could see it there, right under the coaster!! Sure that it was cracked and barely working, we set off to get her a new one. *Never a dull moment.*

While I was there my homie, Catherine, was visiting her dad just south of where Pam lives! We made the trek across the Skyway Bridge, which Pam HATES driving over, but she conquered the fear that day for some fun, in true Pam form.

We paddled on some kayaks through the intercoastal, as two of my worlds collided. Catherine and Pam getting to meet was surreal, but gratitude ran deep as some of my best friends clicked and we all got to genuinely giggle together in such a crazy time in the world. *Keep your friends close. That's the only part of that quote that matters.*

~*~

There started to be news of incentives for getting the Covid vaccine. There were state and government incentives like rides to vaccination sites, free childcare while you were getting the shots and even lottery tickets! With pretty big winnings too!

Other cities and companies were along for the ride as well! If you pulled up to a Krispy Kream donut shop and showed proof of vaccination, you got a free donut! McDonald's was giving menu coupons, and New York City was giving vouchers for Shake Shack if you got the vaccine at a mobile site in the city!

Would you believe that certain dating apps like Match and Tinder, in hopes of somewhat normalizing the new world of online dating, would offer vaccinated users access to "premium content" and profile boosts... *What was the world coming to?!*

~*~

    I couldn't believe it was June already. Time has always and will always blow my mind, especially with how quickly mid 2021 came, in a flash. This intangible thing runs our lives. Something is seriously wrong there. I live for the moments that aren't scheduled, mapped out or at the mercy of time. Make sure to find some of those moments in your life!!

    Becca's about-to-be mother-in-law decided we needed to throw a bridal shower. At first it was going to be just the girls, like a bachelorette party. We ended up collaborating and allowing the boys to be there in our graces. We had a lot of fun setting it up, and getting a zoom meeting happening to include Andrew's family in Chicago. I made breakfast quiches and an array of other snacks. One thing you should know about Becca, is that she LOVES Cheez-Its. I found a big easter basket in her garage and put a giant mixing bowl inside, filled it with her favorite snack and presented it to her. "The Cheez-It Chalice" we called it. One epic picture was snapped of Becca, Andrew and I surrounding the chalice. That picture now lives hanging on my fridge and remains one of my favorites ever. The party was a good segway into the insane amount of work that needed to be done for the wedding. Details won't be shared on that, but you'll get a full rundown later on with the wedding day.

One project we started and somehow, miraculously, managed to finish by September was a giant mural on the side of their garage; a view of a lake through aspen trees in fall, backed by mountains peaked with snow. My initial reaction to her request was, "You should have told me you wanted this done by your wedding right after your proposal!" We had some fun days working on that over the next few months, and if I do say so myself... it came out pretty darn good!

A few days later, a 12 story condominium partially collapsed in Miami in the middle of the night. Unfortunately, it took almost 100 lives in the fall. After some investigation, which continues still, they found that the building had started to slowly sink as early as the 1990's!

With coastal buildings, they had been starting to see that more and more. The ground isn't as sturdy there, as the amount of groundwater is so significant. Who knows what the future holds for those older buildings along coastlines, but I know it has opened some eyes in the architectural world... with good reason!

At the end of June, Canada saw a heatwave that obliterated their previous heat records. For days on end, the temperatures were clocking in at over 120 degrees fahrenheit. Prior to this, this record had never gone above 113 degrees (farenheit). In Vancouver alone, the heat was believed to contribute to the death of 65 people over a 5 day time span. This same intense heat wave also hit the northwestern section of the United States. It was called a "heat dome" and was absolutely miserable for all involved up there!

    These events, which were thought to most likely be due to human-caused climate change, continued. Scientists think that weather patterns like these are becoming more and more dangerous due to the speed at which our climate is changing.

    In the middle of July, record rainfall triggered floods in Europe, killing 220 people in Germany and Belgium within a 3 day time frame. The flooding was described as "biblical"... something about that word strikes a cord when you're describing floods. The images were haunting...roads crumbled, bridges almost nonexistent, full walls of homes and entire buildings ripped away, debris strewn through entire villages.

    Here we go again, Mother Nature, never ceasing, fighting back. I'm pretty sure She hates us.

~*~

Another odd event, one that rattles the mind is that 2021 became the year for "Space Tourism". Remember when astronauts used to be carefully selected for space endeavors based on knowledge of the craft and the destination?

Welp? Billionaires were now funding shuttle launches and hopping along for the ride. Richard Branson was the first to offer and experience a touristic space ride. He was then followed by actor William Shatner and Amazon founder, Jeff Bezos. Elon Musk also launched Space X! There was no sign of stopping there. They had their eyes set on the future of "civilian" space travel. I put that in quotes as something tells me someone wouldn't be able to hop aboard one of those shuttles without 7 or 8 figures lying around. $$$$$

Who would have thought that this would be a thing? What year is it really? Are we in a version of the Twilight Zone?!

Remember way back at the beginning of all of this when the Olympics had been postponed? They were now rescheduled to start July 23rd and run into August. It felt really weird, as all I remember growing up was the Olympics being a huge deal. We made time to sit down and watch many of the events throughout the whole thing.

The production of lights and decorum was always a full spectacle. The audience brought power and emotion to the arenas.

This year was a sad and unfortunate reality due to the ongoing pandemic. There were no families or friends in the stands cheering on the athletes. The arenas were dreary and unexciting. This unfortunately created a spreading event, also.

My only thoughts were about how hopeful I was that somehow, someday we would be able to get back to the Olympics the world used to know and love.

We FINALLY got to enjoy a concert at the world famous Red Rocks Amphitheater near the end of July. It was kind of scary being in a crowd of thousands of people again, but we found a nice little space towards the back to groove. Carter, unfortunately, had to work another event that weekend. As sad as he was to miss it, it was one of his biggest money weeks annually and he was finally back to work after months of concerts not happening. The festival: Global Dance. *Boots 'n' Cats 'n' Boots 'n' Cats.*

Our favorite band, STS9 (Sound Tribe Sector 9), had to cancel their 2020 shows and my emotions ran high that we were able to see them again. Becca and I had started going together years before, but I hadn't missed a Sound Tribe show at Red Rocks since I started seeing them in 2008! It was also her hubby, Andrew's, first time ever seeing them, which always made it more special.

Catherine, our friend Ronnie and my mom all came too. It felt good to roll deep with a fully sober crew to one of my favorite events of the year. Sound Tribe brings heady beats and instrumental jams. Some of my favorite songs include <u>Poseidon</u>, <u>Vapors</u>, <u>Walk To The Light</u>, <u>Totem</u>, <u>Moonsocket</u>, <u>F. Word</u>, <u>Be Nice</u> and <u>Warrior</u>… I could go on and on. Go check out a live Red Rocks set on YouTube. You won't be disappointed!

~*~

In early August, I spent a full week in the mountains to celebrate my mom's birthday and help Becca with wedding preparations. We spent a couple of full days painting the mural and putting bouquet flowers together. Becca had ordered hundreds of wooden flowers, which I loved because now we would have the bouquets forever! We poked each one with a flowering wire and ensured they were going to stay together with some hot glue. Her yard was strewn with colorful flowers and music filled the cool, mountain air. In true fashion, we giggled our way through the entire afternoon while the dogs frolicked around us.

Over the course of the week I glued hundreds of decorative butterflies to clothes pins, which eventually landed in places all around the wedding venue. More on that later.

I made dinner for my mom for her birthday and we had a little game night with one of her friends. The next morning, the power went out while I was working and my mom and I ended up in her closet with the dogs, protecting them from thunder booms that rattled the house. It was funny for us, but the dogs thought differently as they buried their heads in our armpits, scared to death of the intensity of the storm!

Carter and I had been talking about getting a new-used car for some time. It just so happened that a woman my mom knew was selling one. It was completely serendipitous, as I bought it almost immediately after one test drive. The car that Carter had was pushing 400,000 miles, and screamed as it went around any corners or up any hills. We decided to purchase it as our anniversary gift to ourselves, as we celebrated 7 years together. I planned a day for us to spend together driving up to Lookout Mountain, where the views over Denver stretch practically into the Great Plains.

I Google-mapped and found a totally random, extremely tiny park in Golden that I thought would be totally empty, since I randomly picked it off the map. When we got there, the town was holding a bike race and was flooded with people. We ended up in a park closer to home and giggled about my find through Google Maps. We're simple folk, our anniversaries usually consist of a meal at home over a movie rather than getting all dressed up and going out to some fancy place. *My kinda guy.*

On August 28th, we attended a Celebration of Life and memorial for a dear friend. He was a member of my mom's circle and the partner of 18 years to one of her best friends, Nancy. Mark had lost a grueling battle with Pancreatic Cancer.

He was one of the brightest lights I have ever known. You could always catch him in a tie-dye shirt, with his long silver hair pulled back in a ponytail. Every November, he would hold a Scorpio party, as his birthday was on 11/11. The memory of walking into his apartment is clear as though it was yesterday. His walls were lined with vinyl records, CD's, cassette tapes and instruments. All of his closest friends would pile into his tiny living room, sitting on laps and on the floor between knees. He always had a loaded pipe and bowl of weed on the table, free for anyone to enjoy. Each night would consist of yummy snacks, excellent music, marijuana smoke and tequila shots (responsibly). His parties were classy, he would have friends play guitar, tell stories or jokes, and Mark would make sure that every person there got a hug when they came in and a hug when they left. His love for music, his friends and for Nancy was second to none.

He lived so much life in his time here on this earthly plane. You could find him chilling by the record player, teaching us about this artist or another… that was if he wasn't climbing a mountain or at the head of the line for a concert.

His celebration of life was beautiful. Everyone wore purple (the color for Pancreatic cancer awareness) and got to enjoy an afternoon much like his Scorpio parties, minus the marijuana freely flowing. The room was lined with his CD's and records, of which he wished his friends to take home and enjoy in his honor. Everyone enjoyed a shot of Tequila at the end, I held up a bubbly but was emotional all the same. I ended up with The White album by The Beatles and the soundtrack to Fast Times at Ridgemont High, both on vinyl. He was there with us as tears ran and laughter echoed.

Mark, you are, and forever will be, greatly missed. Your light shines on in all of us and we know that you're in the front row at the greatest concert of all time.

~*~

September was carved out for wedding preparations...

But first I got some really fun news! Kalypso had won Pet-Of-The-Month through our vet! They reached out asking for some of my favorite pictures of him and a little blurb for them to post online and put up in their office! I was ecstatic, being that my Kalypso is, of course, the cutest kitty ever! And I have at least a trillion photos of him in my phone just waiting to be shared with the world. I ended up creating his own Instagram account in 2020, and find myself scrolling through it when I am missing him. *I really am pathetic, aren't I? @kalypsaurus if you wanna give him a follow.* He got that name from a stegosaurus haircut I gave him one year. It was epic.

The vet posted a bulletin board in the clinic and made a post on the Facebook page. It made me feel like a proud mamma that my baby was famous for a month. He's been through a lot, he deserves it!

9/11/2021 was the 20 year anniversary. It was really hard to believe it had been that much time since that tragic day. I remember it like it was yesterday, little 5th grade me. A moment of silence and a few deep breaths to remember those that fell with the towers.

...
...
...

I spent basically the first half of the month at Becca's house. We finished the mural, painted signs, and completed bouquets, table centerpieces, and the playlist. A true DIY wedding, and she wouldn't have it any other way. As Maid-Of-Honor, it was my duty to ensure the fairy tale day she dreamt of... it was really happening! Becca was getting hitched!

Dresses had arrived and plans for the rehearsals were in play. We spent the whole day before setting up at the beautiful location on the Colorado River, leaving nothing to do the day of but flip the lights on.

Here we go, the moment I've been waiting for in writing this crazy year for you.

Becca, Ashley, Anna and I (her 2 other longtime friends and bridesmaids) all crowded into the master bathroom where our hair and make-up products covered the countertop. I helped Ashley curl her hair, which she had colored vibrantly. Orange, pink, blue and purple intertwined through her long, thick curls, which were sprayed stiff with hairspray so they didn't come out before the big event. After quickly curling my hair and Becca helping me pin a few pieces back, I went downstairs to solicit Carter's help to get my dress on. I knew it was going to take some shimmying anyway, so I made sure to eat really well and sparingly the week before, so that my dress would without-a-doubt fit. My dress was a raspberry purple, with a lacy diagonal strap, which showcased my favorite tattoo perfectly. I had fall colored glitter french tip nails and stripes of color throughout my hair too, which were spiral curled to perfection and bouncing excitedly just like I was.

    After a successful dressing, I went back upstairs to do my makeup. I was the first one in my dress so everyone gawked as I entered the bathroom. We had an hour until we had to be at the venue, so I did what I could to help hurry the girls along.

    Everyone was looking so beautiful all done up, and I assure you that with this group of girls, it was probably the most make-up any of us had ever worn. I know it was for me, and I had purchased some make-up setting spray because I knew the day would come with lots of tears.

    Time was ticking away...

The boys left for the venue and we got Becca into her dress. It was a tank top style with lacing over the shoulders and cascading down the bust, around her hips and down the back, with a long trailing fabric that would be pinned up for dancing. The back was mesh with buttons up the center, pearly ones with little loop holes to go through. Donna, Becca's grandma, got her buttoned up and then realized one was off, no surprise with that many buttons! I put Becca's back in the sun and followed each loop down until I found the missing one. Of course it was more than half way down. I started undoing them and realized my dang fake nails were too long for this project, I couldn't grip them!

Anna came to the rescue with short nails and tweezers to get her straightened out. The photographer was with us for the whole weekend so every activity and giggle was captured. He snapped a picture of us doing surgery on the dress and then when it was fixed, he captured Becca looking over her shoulder with the sun lighting up the sparkles. It will forever be one of my favorite pictures of her. *My beautiful bestie!* I seriously get emotional thinking about it, which is ridiculous, but emotions were running high that day, of course.

We loaded up in the cars and headed out for AA Barn in Grand Lake. The road out to the barn was lined with aspen trees, and they were at their ultimate peak of colors. Usually in that area, you don't get those deep reds and purples with the leaves, only gold. But some magic was working here because it was the most beautiful I had ever seen. As I parked, I saw the guests mingling over by the altar, which we were calling the "stargate" or the "portal".

Sitting next to the river was a wooden hexagon portal garnished with flowers ranging from white and tan to deep oranges, reds and purples. The aisle leading to the stargate had stumps from local pine trees topped with decorated glass vases wrapped in flowers and butterflies, filled with water and colored beads and floating candles. *E-candles, I should say, as we didn't want to be the cause of yet another fire in Grand Lake. Local kids, we knew better!*

The entrance of the barn held a wooden pallet we had transformed into a scheduling sign. I will just mention, again, how long Becca and I spent on Pinterest narrowing down all the things she wanted, we managed to have just the right amount of decorations.

The sign read:
Welcome
Dating 1.12.19
Engaged 4.12.20
Marriage 9.18.21
Ceremony 2pm
Dinner 4pm
Dancing 6 - ∞

Behind the pallet sign was another small sign reading **Dance Party** with an arrow pointing to the back of the barn. On the other side of the barn entrance were some yard games for the kids, which of course had its own handmade sign. Just beyond that, we had set up their camping canopy to have an "escape room"... you know, in case a moment was needed by any of the wedding party.

We had decked it out with tarp walls, rocking chairs, a rug, table and even string lights!

When Becca showed up, we made a sheet curtain to hide her from being seen and snuck her over to the escape room. Needing to take a moment, we all took a few deep breaths as the groomsmen lined up for the ceremony. We left her in the canopy, as her Grandpa Jack would be escorting her shortly. Lining up, I had to remind myself to breathe, I was being overrun with emotions.

Andrew, the groom, walked his mom and Grandma Donna down the aisle and seated each of them after a hug. Andrew's brother, Kevin, and I walked first with LaLa, their dog, who we had practiced with to stay focused on Andrew as we approached, otherwise she would have been searching desperately for Becca. Kevin was stocked with treats in his pocket also, just to cover any bases of distraction.

I stood next to the portal as Anna and Andrew's other brother, Patrick, came down. I spotted my mom and she instantly calmed me when she smiled, telling me to breathe. She could see me overrun with emotion. Ashley and Andrew's cousin, Dan, came down last and then once we were all in place, Jack walked with Becca down the aisle. I could see her gripping his arm, slowing herself down and keeping her joyous tears at bay.

My god, she looked so beautiful. Tears started to well up in my eyes, but thankfully, LaLa distracted me and got me to giggle when she saw Becca coming down. She stood on her back legs and gave a loving squeal of excitement. She had done that in the rehearsal too and it was perfect.

Grandpa Jack gave Becca a kiss on the cheek and a hug before placing her hand into Andrew's. As she spun to face him, I fixed the shimmering tail of her dress and took LaLa's leash, who laid down right next to Becca's feet, as practiced, perfectly shaded by her parents.

For a unity ceremony, Becca and Andrew planted a spruce tree together. Kevin brought it to them and I picked up a decorated vase for the watering. At the right moment, Becca turned to me, we caught eyes and winked at each other. The photographer captured the moment and that too, remains one of my favorites. They exchanged rings and concluded the ceremony with a kiss and then as they walked through the guests, Andrew dipped Becca for another. Everyone cheered and whooped.

We followed them and then went into the barn, as the guests followed. Becca and Andrew, with LaLa, went to the escape room to "decompress".

It was time to gather for pictures, the wedding party and family. We had photos by the portal, of all of us and then some individual shots with the bride and groom. Shots were snapped of us in the river, which was an experience in itself. Andrew's brother slipped off a rock and got his pant leg wet. I was in tights and got the bottom of those wet. Anna almost fell completely in and the bottom of Becca's dress had a dip too. These genuine moments were captured in time by Jay, the photographer, as he endlessly snapped away.

Becca and Andrew went off to take some pictures in an Aspen grove and we went over to the barn to greet the party and start mingling.

Entering the barn, there was a rose gold balloon spelling **Love** surrounded with tassels and butterflies. Wooden pillars lined the center, wrapped in twinkling fairy lights and littered with clothes-pinned pictures of the newlyweds life, both before union and after...and of course, butterflies.

Continuing through, there was a table with the butterfly clips overflowing out of it, the same basket that we had dubbed the Cheez-It Chalice. A handmade sign said, "Spread the Love! Take a butterfly and pin it." Becca ended up with butterflies all over her dress, fluttering down the lacey bottom tail-piece that was pinned up for her to be able to walk around. I had one in my hair, a few on my dress, the boys all had them clipped to their suit collars and pockets. They ended up pinned all over the venue, everywhere you looked, which was exactly the hope!

Next to that table was where the cake sat. A small white, two-tiered cake with white mountains sat amongst a variety of beautiful cupcakes. Becca had the cake topper made custom. A heart surrounded a silhouette of a couple on a ski chairlift, with a dog between them. It looked just like Becca, Andrew and LaLa. The cupcakes dazzled with candy pearls on lavender frosting and ones with cinnamon sugar glistening in the barn lighting. Jay snapped a picture of me hiding behind a small sign saying "I came for the cake!" *Appropriate.*

As you continued through the barn, a table sat with a colorful activity. The handmade sign read: "Guest Tree - please "leaf" your fingerprint and sign your name in the book with your best wishes."

Becca had painted a tree and had everyone put an ink thumbprint onto it as leaves, a visual guestbook along with one to sign and write in. It turned out so beautiful, all the colors blended so well together. LaLa's paw print even graced it, looking like falling leaves below the branches.

Sitting beautifully in the corner, sat a memorial table. Becca had lost her mom some years back and wished more than anything that she could be at the wedding, so we brought some memorial decorations, pictures of her mom and Andrew's grandpa, lights, candles, a Himalayan Salt lamp and a sign reading, "Because someone we love is in Heaven, there is a little bit of Heaven at our wedding."

Out the back side of the barn, we set up tables with white clothes. Rustic string-Festoon lighting surrounded the tables and dance area. After the ceremony, we moved the decorated vases and sat them on top of the wooden pillars that the lights hung off of. Behind Becca and Andrew's table at the top of the circle, was a white arch decorated with lace and a kaleidoscope of butterflies. *Yes, that is one of the names for a group of butterflies, one of the coolest names for sure!*

Every table had a crafted centerpiece. Andrew had taken slices of a downed local tree, sanded them up and stained them. Sitting on those were small glasses holding glittery candles, butterflies and frilly decorations similar to the aisle vases. *Of course anytime I say candles, I mean electronic ones. Taking no chances.*

After all the work we had put in the day before decorating and the year of preparation, seeing it all completed with dressed up guests and my beautiful bestie bride, made it all so worth it!! We had created the fairy tale wedding we had been working for.

Catering served us beautiful plates of meat, veggies, potatoes and croissants. Completed with some of the tastiest sauce I've ever had, although I couldn't tell you what it was.

I was aware that my Maid-of-Honor speech was after Andrew's father's, so when he got up to speak I was preparing myself and knew I had a little while. I was feeling a little bit anxious and knew I would be emotional throughout it... but I had to eat that fear, for Becca. Of course, her new father-in-law's speech was basically just letting them know he loved them, congratulations and then introducing me... in like 3 minutes. I was not prepared in 3 minutes! I gulped, looked at Becca and

Andrew and stood up to walk to the front of the dance floor.

I literally cried the entire time I was reading... the only good picture of me doing my toast was from the back. I will be the first to admit I am an ugly crier and... what a freaking blub fest. *Here goes!*

"Good evening to our growing family.
I am made-of-honored to be up here, and sharing this evening with you all, to celebrate a new chapter in the lives of 2 wonderful people.

If you have not yet, please be sure to check out the thumbprint tree and guestbook, memorial table, and be sure to pin a butterfly up somewhere, and that one goes home with you!

To say that Becca is my best friend, is an understatement.
Noticing many parallels in our journeys, we have decided to run alongside each other, and I couldn't be more grateful.
Throughout our lives, we have become aligned, woven and bonded at the deepest levels, my soul sister. Not related by blood, but a bond that transcends time, space and distance.

Becca has always been able to bring light into darkness, finding the lessons and laughter in things. She tackles challenges with determination that can not be rivaled and fights hard for her dreams... and for those she cares about. And now, she has her prince charming, who I know she will fight for, as I have seen for myself.

The way these 2 work together to overcome obstacles, make dreams into reality and love each other is both rare and inspiring. Over Becca and Andrew's time together, I have seen immense growth between them. From building a beautiful homestead to the rewarding and challenging lifestyle changes they have made.
Sometimes all you need is one person that shows you it's ok to let your guard down, be yourself, and love with no regrets.

Andrew, getting to know you the last couple years has been a blessing. I have come to love you and your creative ideas, how hard you work and the depth in which you love my girl. I will thank you endlessly.

Becca, life with you is never boring. Our time together brings about colorful ideas, crazy adventures, genuine giggle fits and unintentional word jumbles.
You will always have a piece of my heart.

And Andrew, as you protect and hold Becca's heart, know that a piece of mine rides along as your friend… and her crazy best friend.

Get ready for a wild ride.
She's your beautiful, wonderful, word jumble now.

To the bride and groom.
May your love be boundless."

    I could see that Becca had teared up too. That made me feel better. They both stood and came over to me for a hug. A photo was snapped of Andrew and my hug, me from the back… the only good picture.

    Andrew's brother's speech came after mine, which was a good plan as they were able to make everyone laugh and dry their eyes.

    Dances came next, with an emotional first dance between the bride and groom. I had just fixed my make-up in the escape room, only to cry all over again during their dance. It was slow and passionate. Becca would look into Andrew's eyes and sing him some of the lyrics. When I later watched the video I took, guess what? I cried all over again. Thank goodness for "waterproof" mascara... not totally waterproof but at least I didn't look like a raccoon.

Becca danced with her grandpa and Andrew danced with his mom, then we got to have some fun with our playlist. There was only a small group of us that actually danced, so we ended up standing in a circle and just all vibing out together.

As the sun started to go down, the lights really brought the place to life. The little electric candles lit up the vases and made the flowers and butterflies shimmer. The festoon lighting around the tables and dance floor was just the perfect lighting for this love story, making the old barn feel rustically nostalgic.

It was time for the happy couple to cut their cake. We all made our way into the small barn and gathered as they went around the back. Becca picked up the knife and Andrew placed his hands over hers. They looked at each other and then around at all of us before plunging the knife into the cake. As they fed each other a bite, I could see the guests wondering if they were going to shove it up and down their faces. I knew that they had made an agreement to not uphold that wedding tradition, with good reason as we were basically in the middle of the woods and there was no bathroom with running water for Becca to wash her face and re-apply full make-up. The first test of trust in their marriage… passed.

    After cake and cupcakes, which were freaking delicious by the way, guests started to slowly trickle back to their homes. Once I started to see that, I began to pull some of the things together that we needed to break down… which was actually everything. The entire barn needed to be cleaned out by the end of the night. Becca, the bridesmaids, Carter and I all brought a change of clothes for cleaning up… which none of us ended up changing into, except Carter. He went into full "load-out" mode like he was packing up a concert. *Like a boss.*

    Everyone helped with the breakdown. We made a fire line, bringing everything from the back of the barn to the front and then from there to the cars. The coolers with drinks, all the tablecloths and centerpieces, vases, lighting, speakers and microphone set-up, the fairy lights with the pictures, the memory table, thumbprint tree board, butterflies, the yard games, the space portal/alter, chairs…and all the trash had to go.

Everything was fitting into one car or another, a family affair. We could see the end in sight.

Becca and I ended up emptying giant trash cans together… in our dresses. We giggled about it as there was probably no bride ever, emptying trash juice out in her stunning wedding dress and her Maid-of-Honor helping her do it in her own gown.

The day had been a fairy-tale success. Becca's vision was brought to life. From proposal to the first planning session, spending hours on Pinterest and researching DIY weddings. It had all fallen right into place just the way we had imagined. My bestie was hitched.

~*~

    The first weekend of October, Carter and I flew to Oklahoma for a celebration of life for his Grandpa Gene. He had an immensely full life.

    Gene Redman III loved to dance, and would use the expression that he "had more moves than a bucket full of worms"! He spent years playing football and spent many of them as varsity captain! Gene went on to be a teacher when he ended up in Colorado, teaching history, P.E. and geography, as well as coaching multiple sports teams! He coached and judged in the Junior Special Olympics for many years and he found joy in helping young people build self esteem, character and confidence. *We could use some more people like that in the world today!*

    When he retired he taught driver's education and went on to establish a driving program with AAA, then went on to driving buses for the Denver Public Transport! He loved education and loved his family more than anything. This exudes from Carter's mom, aunt and uncle. They were brought up by the best to be hard working and hard loving, ensuring family is among the top priorities in their lives. *I feel so lucky to be a part of this family.*

I had to prepare myself for this full family reunion, but was graciously and warmly welcomed.

We gathered at a church and did a small ceremony with some cookies, fruit and a beautiful photo collage of Gene and the family on a projected screen. Afterwards, we all met for dinner at a local Italian restaurant. The Redman clan was rolling 25 strong. We took up the entire back wall of the dining room and came hungry. Aromas tickled my nose as the servers placed warm bread and oil and vinegar for dipping. I was indulging, a celebration to my tummy for having to eat well to fit in my bridesmaid dress. Another piece of bread soothed my soul. Although, after I devoured my raviolis too, I was over stuffed.

The next day we gathered at his cousin's house just around the corner from the hotel. A large garden and lawn gave way to a roundabout driveway. As we drove up, a big dog came to greet us, named Mia, same name as our kitty at home! She had a deep bark, but after her initial guard duty, gave off serious loving vibes, drool and all. We walked through the gate into the pool and pool house area. A copper mermaid greeted us with her horn spouting water and the familial greetings began. Carter had cousins, aunts, uncles, and even second cousins at this party! We ate great food, played games and enjoyed the beautiful new-school Victorian home. I made friends with their other animals too… of course. A smaller heeler mix pup, who had an adorable grin and their kitty who had a purr-fectly curled french mustache in his fur pattern. I can remember neither of their names and upon asking some of the family, they couldn't either.

    As the sun was going down, the backyard lit up with beautiful lighting and the pool lights changed colors. It was warm and not too humid, so sitting outside for dinner was perfect. After again eating way too much food, we were blessed with the opportunity to just relax in our room. The bed engulfed me. Food-comatose. I woke up in the early hours to Ancient Aliens playing on the TV, which is what we went to sleep watching.

    It was a short trip, having to leave right after breakfast the next day to drive back down to Dallas to catch our flight home. One thing is for sure though, Grandpa Gene's spirit was surrounding us all weekend. We even threw some Lindberg chocolates and Chocolate Pecan cookies into the celebration, for good measure, his favorite.

    October 7th was the 7 year anniversary of my dad's passing. That day always grounds me in how grateful I am to be sober. So many opportunities have come to me through recovery. I feel truly blessed.

If you or someone you know is struggling with alcohol or substance use, encourage them to seek support. **Tell them you love them. I know the stigma around addiction and mental health runs deep, but I assure you... there is support. Overcoming that first step in seeking help paves a way for wonderful things to happen. Life can hold so much joy, and trust me... there is fun to be had sober. Sounds crazy now, but I promise it's worth exploring.

Over Halloween weekend, one of my longtime favorite bands, Ween, was doing a 3-day run in Denver. Carter was the stage manager that weekend, and he always brags that he has the best job when they come to town because he gets to pull the stage reveal of their logo, called the "Boognish". WEEN!!!

They're funky and weird as hell. We've all been listening to them since high school, 2006 to be exact and they always bring a giant group of us together. There have been some shows at Red Rocks that we've had like 60 of us together. *We roll deep.*

Anyway, my homie, Lauren, and I met up at my house, both dressed in sequins... unplanned. We got a sweet spot on the venue's balcony and ended up meeting up with a few peeps. Ween crushed it, playing almost everything I wanted to hear, but I still decided to go the next night too.

    I decided a long time ago that I wasn't going to attend shows on Halloween night anymore, after a couple weird ones. Something about all the costumes, a dark and loud environment, and the vibe of those mixed doesn't sit well with me. The years I have been sober have left me eating candy at home, and I have no problem with that at all. However, when Ween comes to town, it would be a disservice as a fan to skip the shows and devour an entire bag of mixed chocolates instead.

    *If you have never heard of Ween, I suggest you listen to the following songs: <u>Ocean Man</u>, <u>Transdermal Celebration</u>, <u>Exactly Where I'm At</u>, <u>The Mollusk</u>, <u>Stay Forever</u>, <u>A Tear for Eddie</u> and <u>Tried and True</u>. *Man, isn't YouTube great?!*

    Enjoy!

~*~

November. Whew! Almost through the 2nd year of this craziness. Some more stories and some statistics will conclude this story. Let me just say I have truly enjoyed writing this for you as my reader, and I hope you have equally enjoyed reading it.

Catherine came to hang out for a weekend in the mountains in early November. She brought her pup, Zeus. Catherine, Zeus, Buddy and I enjoyed a day working from home together and then got to play over the weekend. We had beautiful weather, ate good nutritious food, and had some serious giggles to fill in any gaps.

On Sunday, we took the dogs out for a walk in the woods. Buddy and Zeus lapped us and played like puppies. Buddy got really excited and tried to zoom around all of us, got caught up in a completely rusted barbed wire fence and it flipped him over, sending him tumbling.

I gasped! Buddy hopped up and kept running. I managed to get him over to me in his excitement and observed his legs for any cuts. All good, no blood!

We continued the walk and as we were coming around the corner to my mom's house, after over an hour of running around, Buddy stopped and was licking his leg up by his inner shoulder.

Walking over to him, I noticed a little blood. Bending over and carefully grabbing his leg to take a closer look, I came across a 1.5 inch gash in his leg. Deep. Like down to the vein deep! I could SEE it! *Do dogs need tetanus shots? What if he bleeds out? Is that an artery? This would happen when my mom is half way across the country!*

Thank a higher power that Catherine was there, my animal hero! She said that dogs have a vein right there and that he needed to, no doubt, get stitched up.

I swear, my anxiety would have riddled me at this moment. Catherine may never know how grateful I am that she was there… unless she reads this book! Just her presence and experience with animals ensured me that both Buddy and I were in good hands.

Buddy limped and we slowly walked the rest of the way to the house. I had him lay outside, gave him some water and started calling around to find a vet who might be available on a Sunday afternoon.

My mom was in Florida at the time and her phone was off, so I called my aunt. Of course my mom was in the middle of receiving a massage, but this was urgent enough for my aunt to let her know what was going on.

Thinking about this makes me grateful that no one burst into my massage room when my apartment was flooding (at the very beginning of this story), but if it had to do with my animal, I most definitely would have wanted someone to. That was my logic here.

I have so much gratitude to Dr. Brooks for answering the phone and helping us out on a Sunday late afternoon. Buddy was so good, probably because I fed him treats the whole way to the vet to keep him from licking his wound. It was a quick visit. Some antibacterial powder, 4 staples, another treat and we were on our way back home. Dr. Brooks prescribed 10 days of oral antibiotics and orders to dress him in a shirt for 2 weeks to keep him from licking the wound or removing the staples.

Buddy looked too cute in his little long sleeve shirt with rolled up sleeves, but I had to watch him carefully because he kept sticking his perfect little nose up into the sleeve attempting to get to those staples.

He's all healed up now, but I was planning to go into the woods during the summer with big ol' wire cutters and pull out all that rusty wiring so that this doesn't happen to anyone else or their pup!

~*~

Carter's family came out for Thanksgiving and we enjoyed a super cozy dinner with all nine of us in his uncle's tiny apartment. My mom makes the best cranberry sauce ever, her grandmother's recipe, so we were tasked with bringing that, as well as some roasted veggies and green bean casserole. Carter's whole family loves that cranberry sauce!

Our holiday began. The trip to his Uncle Gene's was about an hour, so we loaded everything up and headed out to eastern Colorado.

As we were all enjoying our appetizers, my mom froze. The blood drained from her face, as she said "Oh f**k!!" and then proceeded to tell us that she realized she had forgotten the cranberry sauce in our fridge. Her eyes darted to Carter and me, in high hopes that one of us had grabbed it.

Unfortunately, we had already come to terms with the fact that it was still sitting back in the fridge in Denver, a bit too far to go back for! None of us showed how sad we were, so as to not make her feel any worse about it than she already did.

I could read her face though and saw that she was really bummed about it. To try to remedy it, I told her we could go find something that could replace it, since you can't have Thanksgiving dinner without cranberry sauce or something similar.

We were in a tiny little town with one small grocery store and a Dollar General. The grocery was closed so we tried our luck in the dollar store. My innovative mind had to kick in because the food shelves were barren. I found a package of fruit cups that contained peaches and cranberries in gelatin… "It works". We swooped up the package and headed back to the apartment. I was happy I was able to make her giggle at the situation because I could tell it was upsetting her.

Dinner was amazing, with the smoothest mashed potatoes I've ever had, I don't know what the secret is and that's ok. Topping my stomach off with chocolate cream pie sent me into a full food coma. Another successful holiday with the family, even with the cranberry sauce fiasco. Thankfully, everyone got to enjoy it with their leftovers the next day back in Denver. My mom promised everyone that would never happen again.

~*~

Holy crap people, December… again! My original thought was to write only about 2020, but at some point in 2021, I realized that with all the crazy things that continued to happen, the story was not over. Besides, going to bed before the new year and missing the fireworks just wouldn't have been a very exciting ending to this crazy story. So here goes…

    I was in the mountains for my birthday week. I had picked up a side job as a taxi to and from the airport for a mother and her son who were visiting Winter Park. I brought them up from the airport and was scheduled to take them back down four days later, which happened to be on my birthday, but I didn't mind since I needed the extra cash.

    Becca and I made cupcakes for my birthday, chocolate with raspberry filling and espresso frosting. Talk about a buzz - well, relatively. They were super rich, which was actually good because it kept me from eating more than one at a time!

I had planned a girl's night on my birthday with some friends in the city, so I was packed up and ready to go the night before. A huge storm came in and the prediction was that it would be setting record wind speeds in the city, like 120 mph. This is, thankfully, not another derecho story. However, flights were being canceled all over and there was a downright blizzard happening in the mountains.

After speaking with the mother early that morning, they decided to hop on an airport shuttle and save me the treacherous drive. "Thank goodness for small miracles!" My mom was very relieved also. I happily decided to stay in the mountains and work that day, rescheduled my girls date, and sat sipping tea and watching it snow and blow in the forest outside the office window.

Guess what?!... My cousin Rikki was in Colorado, of course a blizzard would come. She was planning on taking the train up from the city and ended up stuck for hours halfway between Denver and Winter Park, due to high winds. The train went back to the station, what a bust. I was planning on surprising her since I stayed in town!

My mom and I decided to go hit the mountain the following morning since Mary Jane, part of the ski area, was opening for the first day of the season with more than a foot of fresh snow for us to whoop it up in! I will NEVER be mad getting stuck in the mountains. It ended up being quite the perfect birthday; a snowstorm is a gift I will always be thankful for. Much better to ski in it than drive in it!!

    Here's where it gets crazy.
    Over the course of only 3 days.

    On December 27th, a shooting spree in Denver left 5 dead and 3 injured, including a police officer, leaving 7 separate crime scenes in its wake. The suspect also died after gun fire was exchanged, right where Becca and I used to live and work.
    It all started late afternoon at a tattoo parlor, leaving 2 women dead and another man injured. One of the women was a well known artist in the Denver tattoo scene and a friend of a few people I knew, which made it too close to home. The shooter's second stop was actually at another tattoo shop that he had owned some years ago! Who would have ever thought that shootings would happen at tattoo shops?! A chilling realization to the world we are living in.

He then continued to the shopping area where I used to live and then went to hide in a neighboring hotel, shooting a clerk and then a police officer before he was shot and killed. Sadly, the suspect had been known by the police and it was said that they were aware of his extremist views, as well as mental episodes in his past.

My heart goes out to all of their families. Mental health is something that we need to spend much more time talking about and doing something about in this country, as by doing so, who knows how many lives could be saved. Denver came together strong on this and held a fundraiser for the tattoo shops, the victims and their families. That's one beautiful thing about the community in our city, and Colorado, we help our own.

On the 30th, 2 fires broke out in Boulder County in the late morning. Middle Fork fire was swept under the rug, as it was much smaller and contained fairly quickly, as the Marshall Fire ripped ruthlessly through suburban neighborhoods.

The wind was blowing fiercely that day, gusts up to 115 miles per hour were recorded, and I could see the smoke starting to build up from my window in Denver that afternoon. By the time it got dark, I was glued to the live coverage of the Marshall fire. With the high winds, the fire was rolling too fast for anyone to comprehend. Reverse 911 calls were made as quickly as possible but many lost their homes within just a couple of hours, not even enough time to return from work to gather belongings or animals. This was a relentless fury of flames.

In just a day's time, the fire consumed over 1000 structures, including homes, a hotel, the museum and a shopping center. Colorado is "used to" (not exactly the right terminology there) fires running wild in the mountains and burning forests, but we had never seen anything like this in a suburban area. Within 12 hours, this fire claimed the title of the most destructive fire in Colorado history.

We broke 3 fire records in 2 years in our state. It's sad and scary that things could continue to spiral as Mother Nature fights back against us.

The cause of the Marshall Fire was in debate. Downed power lines were the first thought, as it had been an extremely dry winter thus far and high winds could have easily knocked them down. After the fire had extinguished, underground fires in coal mines were found and that was also thought to be a possible cause. As of February 2022, the exact cause was still unknown.

On New Years Eve and into the 1st day of 2022, heavy snowfall put an end to the fires, just a couple days too late.

As I recall, this story started with monumental fires, ended with record breaking fires, and contained some in the middle. I am finding biblical trends here, scared of what is next.

To finish up this year, TV icon, comedian and Golden Girl Betty White passed away. A legend. She spent her life bringing smiles to our faces and worked hard in animal welfare. She started her career on the radio at the age of 8 and went on entertaining us for 9 decades through TV as well as some film directing!

She will be remembered always, her sparkling blue eyes and adorable giggle will live on timelessly through her movies and TV shows that she graced us with over the course of her long life. We can learn a lesson from Betty's life, live every single moment to the absolute fullest.

~*~*~*~*~*~*~

We weren't out of the woods by any means and by the end of 2021 the world had seen over 5 million deaths from the virus and that number was still, unfortunately, rising. By early May, 2022, Covid had claimed over one million lives in the United States. By August 2022, Covid still ran rampant through the world, still being talked about, still creating forceful exercised caution! There were still conspiracies, still controversies on masking and vaccinating, politics and any other thing you could think of for humans to fight about. *Shocker, huh?*

The world is crazy, Mother Nature is fighting back. We are responsible for taking matters into our own hands and making the changes that need to be brought about. Please do your part!

~*~

As I started to think about the closing of this story, emotions started to come up in regard to the reality of how big these last couple of years were. So much happened, but it came with so many lessons.

Your health could be in jeopardy at any moment, same with those you care about. The home that you have filled with things all your life could be literally ripped away by wind, flooded or turned to ashes with very little notice. Your town could be swept away by water, crops and livelihoods ripped away, belongings blown to pieces. Your friends' and favorite artists' lives could be taken…A grim reality, a horrible truth.

What can we take away from this, these insane years?

The biggest lessons I have learned and something that sits within my head and heart is… BE A GOOD HUMAN!! Take care of those around you, and take care of yourself and your space. Cherish the moments in your home, with your animals and family. Give yourself some grace, be grateful for what you have. Take time to make memories with people you love, tell them how you feel, stand up for what you believe in! Take charge of your life and your personal serenity. Spend time in nature, open your heart to any possibility. Time is unreal, unable to be retained, stopped, rewound. Don't let the hurt of the past define you, but remember the lessons that came from it, remember the memories you've made. Spend time in the present and work towards a better future!

Learn about YOU, what makes you tick, what brings you joy?
Those little moments and little things matter! Follow your heart and what you know to be your highest truth.

I want you to know that I am holding space for you, wherever you may be, reading this story.

Thank you.

I leave you with a few quotes, that I have found to be undeniably true:

Don't let the darkness from your past block the light and joy of your present. What happened is done, stop giving time to things which no longer exist when there is so much joy to be found here and now. - Karen Salmansohn

No matter what kind of challenges or difficulties or painful situations you go through in your life, we all have

something deep within us that we can reach down and find the inner strength to get through them. - Alana Stewart

Don't wait for things to get easier, simpler or better. Life will always be complicated. Learn to be happy, right now! Otherwise, you'll run out of time. -Unknown

The End-ish...

I'd like to hear from you!
Follow me and see pictures from these adventures, future endeavors and more on Instagram! ***@BoognishRise***
Follow Kalypso's story ***@Kalypsaurus***

Write to me! I am here if you need someone to vent to, hold space for you, or if you want to tell me about how these stories affected you, changed you, or taught you!
One.Foot.In.Front.9@gmail.com

*With Love & Light,
Mikkilee*